SWORDSMAN'S COMPANION

COMPANION

A Manual for Training with the Medieval Longsword

Guy WINDSOR
THE SCHOOL OF EUROPEAN SWORDSMANSHIP, HELSINKI

Chivalry Bookshelf

The Swordsman's Companion:
A Manual for Training with the Medieval Longsword

Guy Windsor

Published in the United States by
The Chivalry Bookshelf,
3305 Mayfair Lane, Highland Village, Texas, USA 75077
tel. 866.268.1495 (US), fax 978.418.4774.
http://www.chivalrybookshelf.com

Copyright © 2004 Guy Windsor & The Chivalry Bookshelf
    Photographs except 5.4 and figure 10 (Guy Windsor) © 2004 Jari Pallari
Book Design by Brian R. Price
ISBN: 1-891448-41-2
2nd Printing, Printed in India

Windsor, Guy (1973-)

Neither the author nor the publisher assumes any liability for the use or misuse of information contained in this book, nor do the authors or publishers encourage the use of martial arts techniques other than for personal development and historical study. Study of historical martial arts can be dangerous and should only be practiced under the guidance of a qualified instructor.

Contents

For James, Paul, JT and Num:
Brothers in Arms

About the Author

Guy Windsor began training in martial arts at the age of twelve, and specifically in fencing at thirteen. In 1993 he began to practice historical fencing, and in 1994 founded the Dawn Duellists Society (DDS) in Edinburgh, with Paul Macdonald. After completing a Masters degree in English Literature, he trained and worked as an antiques restorer and cabinet maker, while teaching at the DDS. In March 2001 he moved to Finland to open the School of European Swordsmanship, Helsinki (SESH) (http://www.swordschool.com), and since then has taught historical fencing full-time. Within a few months, the School had grown to the point where it became necessary to open a permanent Salle dedicated to the practice of historical European swordsmanship.

Photo credit SNW

Acknowledgements

I would like to acknowledge the following people for their impact on this book. I would have had nothing worthwhile to say without the instruction I have received from the following people:

Gail and Alan Rudge, my first fencing coaches; Prof. Bert Bracewell, a great fencing coach, who encouraged my forays into the older weapons; Steve Fox, whose aphorisms probably fill this book: his explanations of martial arts theory have been fundamental to my understanding; Paul Macdonald, long-time friend and co-founder of the Dawn Duellists Society, with whom I started the whole "real swordfighting" thing back when we both knew nothing; Stefan Dieke for his elucidation of German longsword fencing and Bob Charron who taught me a great deal about Fiore's system.

Geo Cameron Trevarthen, friend and mentor, was the first person to tell me that I really should write this stuff down; without her guidance and support, this book would never have happened. Merja Polvinen, whose indefatiguable support, expert research assistance and critical reading of innumerable early drafts made the project possible. Martin Page, friend and fellow sword-swinger, is largely responsible for making this manual intelligible, and for pushing me to get on and write the damned thing. His technical-writing expertise has been invaluable, as has his historical and esoteric knowledge. Brian Price and Greg Mele whose many editorial corrections and suggestions have been vital. Prof. Ronnie Jack, of Edinburgh University, for checking the Italian Masters chapter. Mrs. Jeanette Acosta Martínez for her assistance with the fencing principles chapter. L. Hermes Michelini, who allowed a stranger to use his work, in a manner typical of the best of the western martial arts community. Sujit Wings, Sari Polvinen, and Stephen Hand for reading drafts and giving expert advice. Ville Virtanen for checking my physics. Auri Poso for establishing a working relationship between me and my word-processor, and doing the callouts. Jari Pallari, for taking the photographs and not being satisfied with second-best. Ilkka Hartikainen for digital photographic work. Lars Wirzenius, for initial photographic work. Jani Hyväri, who drew the illustrations. Topi Mikkola, Provost of the Helsinki branch, who took up the slack at SESH while I was tired, overworked and generally not on the ball due to writing this book. And last but not least my students, without whom there would be no School, and I would be no instructor. I have been exceptionally lucky in the calibre of the students that have chosen to train with me. They are a constant stimulus to my own training, and they have helped enormously in the refinement and codification of my fencing and teaching method.

To all of the above, my heartfelt thanks.

Chapter 1

INTRODUCTION

How to Use This Book

There are many people beginning the study of Western swordsmanship, particularly with the longsword, who have never been taught the basics of body mechanics, footwork, and fencing principles. Discussion threads on various internet fora show that the majority of people interested in this weapon do not have a common language to describe the various actions, nor do they have the kind of basic training that would allow their research into the historical sources to really bear fruit. This book is primarily written for such beginners, to provide them with a solid foundation from which to start making themselves into swordsmen. It is a training manual, containing all the basic theory and technical exercises necessary to get a solid grounding in the use of the longsword. The history of the weapon, an overview of the historical sources for the method of fencing that I teach, and advice on how to maximise the effectiveness of your practice, are also covered. It is assumed that the reader has no training in any martial art, so this book includes everything you need to know about how to train: from a comprehensive warm-up to constructing a training schedule.

This book is not intended to include every possible longsword technique, and it is not intended to be a recreation of the method of any given historical master. Instead, it attempts to provide you with the complete grammar, basic vocabulary, and key phrases of the language of longsword fencing.

I must emphasise here that the method contained in these pages is mine, based on my own understanding of swordsmanship, backed up by my research and experience. I have had many excellent instructors in other weapons, and I hope I shall not disgrace them: while I gratefully acknowledge their contribution to my training, they are not responsible for the theory, exercises, and underlying martial philosophy that I teach.

Before you begin, you must establish what your goals are. People are motivated to train by a huge variety of stimuli and in my experience, it makes no difference what that initial stimulus was. So if you want to become Sir Lancelot, Aragorn, Luke Skywalker, or Conan the Barbarian, then fine, enjoy. Use that fantasy to inspire, but not direct, your training. It can be helpful at times to get back in touch with why you started training in the first place. Just don't expect the techniques you have seen on the screen to be applicable in reality. Ultimately, most people train for the improvement of their physical and mental health (which includes for most people a degree of fantasy enactment), and because the process itself is rewarding.

To begin your study, read the book through, and decide for yourself whether you want to proceed with the long and laborious (but fun, challenging, rewarding, and ultimately glorious) process of making sense of the exercises and the theory of historical swordsmanship. Though the theory comes first, a full understanding of it is impossible unless you have actually made it work in the exercises; likewise, the exercises are unlikely to yield good results if they are not approached with sound theory in mind.

Then set aside a time, preferably each day, of at least 30 minutes, but not more than two hours, to go through the basic exercises in order. Always start with the warm-up to make sure you are in reasonably good condition, and to get used to following instructions. You may want to speak the instructions slowly into a tape-recorder, leaving space between each instruction for you to accomplish the set task, and play that as you practice.

Work your way slowly through the entire solo practice section before attempting the pair work. You may think you are ready but until you can do the solo exercises with ease and fluency, there will be no point moving on. It is very dangerous to rush your training, however keen you are to get on to the "fun stuff". The more attention you pay to the foundations, the taller and stronger the ultimate structure can be.

It will become necessary in time to have a training partner, or even better, a group. Be careful to get on with the actual training: do not get sidetracked into discussions.

In every training session, however advanced you think you are, make sure to revisit the basic body mechanics and footwork exercises. I hope that this book will be used as the basis of your practice. The term manual literally means that which is held in the hand, not that which is kept on a shelf. So keep the book handy, and refer to it whenever you come across a problem. Most beginner problems come from not having fully understood or assimilated the original instruction. It is amazing how often I will tell a given student, for example "during this technique, push your hands forward and it will work better." Months later, the student will tell me "I was practicing that technique, and it just clicked: all I needed to do was push my hands forward more!" So, refer to the exact wording of the explanation of each technique.

The title for this book is a homage to Donald McBane's smallsword treatise, *The Expert Sword-man's Companion*, the first original treatise that I ever handled. It is an inspiring read by one of the most colourful characters in Western swordsmanship history. I hope that this book may do for your practice what his did for mine.

You might well ask who I think I am to be writing a book about the technical use for a weapon I have not been taught to use. To answer that question, read the book. In it, I will either establish myself as an instructor worth my hire, or a charlatan. You decide.

Stage Combat, Re-enactments, SCA and LARP

There are many arenas in which a purely martial approach to practice is not appropriate. Many people involved in re-enactment, stage combat, or live-action roleplay may find this book helpful in that it shows how the longsword should be used according to its original function: killing people. However, many of the techniques that can be safely practiced by martial artists using modern protective equipment are far too dangerous and far too subtle for re-enactment or stage combat.

The main function of stage combat is to provide a thrilling spectacle for the audience. Done well, stage combat can also be reasonably accurate from a martial perspective, and of course is often used to establish characterisation, or to move the plot forwards. There are, at base, two kinds of stage combat system: the adapted martial art, and the purely theatrical method. The former requires that the actors be highly trained martial artists, who just make everything a bit bigger and a bit more flashy, so that the audience will see it. The latter is often based on sport-fencing, but with no real understanding of European martial arts, and therefore the weapons are used inaccurately. A classic example is the stage-rapier fight, which is often made up of about 80% cut-parry-cut: anyone who has studied historically accurate rapier fencing knows that 90% of rapier attacks are with the point. I have never seen the longsword used correctly on stage or screen, except in displays put on by historical martial arts groups.

For the stage-combatant, this book can provide the core of a training method that will at least get them to move like a martial artist, and give them an idea of the available techniques that they can string together to make a safe, exciting fight. It is much easier to direct a fight between two martial artists than between two untrained actors. Of course, there is always the temptation to dumb down. Perhaps 99% of the people who go to see a film that has sword-fights in it can't tell the difference between good technique and bad. But my colleagues and I are working to change that; I hope that one day the audience will demand the same degree of martial realism in a fight as it demands visual realism in special effects.

The re-enactment of historical battles is an excellent pursuit. It is basically unrehearsed stage combat with a huge cast. It provides the opportunity for the re-enactors to wear shiny kit, tool up with swords and have a damn good bash, and for the general public to have a glimpse of history that is far more immediate and present than a book or a film. It must be remembered that the prime function of re-enactment is not the practice of historically accurate fighting methods. War without wounds and slaughter cannot be historically accurate. In fact, the most common historical battlefield techniques are almost universally outlawed on the re-enactment field, and rightly so. The organisation of a safe, dramatic re-enactment, with sometimes thousands of untrained people all fighting at once, usually with no face protection, is, frankly, a miracle. Whenever I have attended such events I have always been surprised by the amazingly few casualties. However, it is certainly the case that a well-trained Western martial artist will provide a better, safer spectacle than the untrained weekend warrior. I would advise any re-enactor reading this to practise all the techniques in this book. Bear in mind also that there is a fundamental difference between fighting alone and fighting in a line. Do not expect to have room to whirl the sword around. In many re-enactments head-attacks and close quarters techniques are illegal: be certain that you fully understand the rules of the society organising the event. You do not need to fear that training in dangerous techniques might make them spontaneously emerge to injure someone in "the heat of battle." There should be no "heat of battle" for a trained martial artist at a re-enactment: it is just fun for you and the crowd.

The Society for Creative Anachronism is, as its name suggests, in general far removed from actual historical combat. Its members use rattan sticks with sword-handles to have a jolly good bash with whatever weapons or combinations seem like fun. Much of the technique in this book can be adapted to SCA fighting, but bear in mind that steel behaves differently to rattan.

I have never participated in a live-action roleplay game, though many of my students do so, and we have given demonstrations and lectures at LARP events. For our purposes there are two LARP scenarios that this book might help you with: pre-ordained fights with steel, and boffer-fighting. A free fencing bout with steel weapons, minimal or no protective gear, but a pre-arranged winner, is quite easy to do if both combatants are trained, preferably in the same system. With practice comes control, and an understanding of how a real fight might progress: training can add realism and ease to these fights. Boffer fighting, however, breaks all the known rules of swordplay. The training should help, but do not be surprised if you get hammered, even if you have been practising with steel weapons for a while. The reasons for this should become obvious when you start training with steel.

Another major difference between historical fencing practiced as a martial art and the above activities is the length of time you need to train before you are considered competent by your peers. I have had a student come up to me at the end of his second class to tell me that he had decided to cease training because he found "fighting with steel too limiting." Needless to say, he had not yet even begun partner drills with steel, but his LARP background had led him to expect a free-for-all in the first class. The plain fact of the matter is that there are far more possible techniques, counters and variations in true historical fencing with steel blades than there are in stage-combat, re-enactment, rattan sword fighting and boffer play put together. Finally it is up to you to decide what parts of this system can be applied in your own arena.

What Are Martial Arts?

There are sports based on martial arts, there are spiritual/meditative systems based on martial arts, and there are even computer games based on martial arts. The original goal of organised martial systems was usually to train soldiers to be able to execute the orders of his superior. That meant being able to kill other people with whatever weapon you happened to have. It did not, I suspect, take long before someone realised that that superior could be yourself. Not the lying, cheating, greedy scumbag most people are at least some of the time, but the ideal self that we all aspire to become. So the external discipline could be internalised, and the practice developed beyond a merely practical method for training soldiers to a more refined system for training the whole individual.

This has led, particularly in modern times, to martial arts styles that are really designed and marketed as self-improvement courses, leading ultimately (one hopes) to a state of enlightenment. At the same time, what with man's ludic nature, allied to a thirst for bloody spectacle, with a whole load of cupidity thrown in, the martial arts have also been co-opted as sports and entertainment, ranging from the public butchery of Christians in Rome, to the frantic flailing of modern sport fencing.[1]

I see martial arts as having five poles: the practical killing system, the spiritual development system, the sport, the spectacle, and the improvement of health. Each has much to recommend it. However, at any pole, something is lost: a system designed purely for killing is worth practising only if you are actually expecting to use it: in that case, best join the army. If the focus of the practice is entirely spiritual, then you might as well go to church. If winning is all that matters, then why not a sport like the 100 metre sprint, or throwing the javelin. If you just want to look good and put on a show, be an actor or a rock star. And there are many other ways to live more healthily. A true martial art must retain something of all of these: it must be practical, it must lead to spiritual development, it must clearly differentiate between skill-levels, it must be aesthetically rewarding, and it must lead to improved health. Many modern martial artists, quite rightly disgusted with the utter lack of style shown in the sporting arena, and the utter lack of practicality shown on the stage, have dismissed these two poles as unworthy. However, I would say that any fencing match between masters that I have seen has been better spectacle than the best stage combat, and (at the highest level of fencing that I have partaken in, anyway), it has always been clear who would have won if the fencers were interested in competition. And of course, every technique used was thoroughly practical (if occasionally made more complex than necessary to better examine the fundamental truths behind the simpler, more street-effective techniques), and each fencer trained to better themselves.

The fifth pole, health, is generally ignored by practitioners of Western (and many Eastern) martial arts. In my grandfather's house (he was a medical doctor, who fenced into his eighties, and lived to be 92) hung a framed piece of calligraphy, which is now on my wall at home. It paraphrases George Silver's *Paradoxes of Defence*. The original reads:

> I speak not against Maisters of Defence indeed, they are to be honoured, nor against the Science, it is noble, and in mine opiniõ[2] to be preferred next to Diuinitie; for as Diuinitie preserveth the soule from hell and the diuell, so doth this noble Science defend the bodie from wounds & slaughter. And moreouer, the exercising of weapons putteth away aches, griefes, and diseases, it increaseth strength, and sharpneth the wits. It giueth a perfect iudgement, it expelleth melancholy, cholericke and euill conceits, it keepeth a man in breath, perfect health, and long life. It is unto him that hath the perfection thereof, a most friendly and comfortable companion when he is alone, having but only his weapon about him. It putteth him out of feare, & in the warres and places of most danger, it maketh him bold, hardie and valiant.[3]

This encapsulates for me most of the benefits of training.

The general health benefits of physical training are well known, including increased strength, increased cardiovascular capability, and weight management. In my opinion, it is also necessary for a martial artist practising ways of hurting people (in however an enlightened and non-violent a fashion) to counter-balance their skill in inflicting injury with skill in healing. This is not only useful for dealing with the stresses and strains of normal training, and the routine bumps and bruises of friendly combat, but also provides a psychological counter-measure to the otherwise constant emphasis on hitting people.

My students eventually progress through the five poles: first the practical martial skills, then the medical skills (which at my School includes remedial massage, breathing exercises, basic nutrition and some use of medicinal herbs); then developing the aesthetic appreciation of swordsmanship; then competitive (as opposed to purely academic) freeplay; and finally the meditative, spiritual aspects of the Art. Naturally, this book is largely confined to practical fencing techniques, but keep in mind that a true martial art partakes of all poles and is limited to none.

WESTERN MARTIAL ARTS

Martial arts exploded into western public awareness in the sixties, a result both of the New Age search for spiritual guidance (almost exclusively from Eastern sources), and the extraordinary popularity of kung-fu movies (spearheaded by Bruce Lee). With the increase in interest in European weapons coming a decade or so later, it was inevitable that some of the have-a-go heroes would begin to attempt to recreate the historical methods of using their weapons. This has, unsurprisingly, been met with limited success.[4] To understand a martial art for which there are very few representatives of a living tradition requires the ability to interpret treatises that were often deliberately obscure, and do not usually cover the very basics of footwork, exact body-mechanics, how to cut, etc.

We are now in the middle of a renaissance in western (i.e. European) martial arts. For a few decades now, perfectly normal people have been strapping on armour and bashing their mates on a Saturday afternoon.[5] What began as a bit of fun has become a massive international groundswell: for the first time since the seventeenth century, craftsmen can earn their keep making swords and suits of armour for use, not just decoration.

Western martial arts, in particular swordsmanship, has this great advantage over so many others: no-one takes it up because they expect to use it in earnest some day. Who carries a sword in the Inner Cities? So we have not had to worry much about thugs looking for cool new ways to hurt people. But the lack of immediate applicability might seem to take away the purpose of the Art. Furthermore, other aspects of the Art seemed to have been covered by other systems. The New-Age types looking for spiritual awareness were all doing Yoga, T'ai Chi Chüan (actually thoroughly lethal and street-effective if taught that way) or Aikido (also not bad on the street if you really know what it's about) the sportsmen and fitness types were doing judo, sport-fencing or aerobics, the actors were on stage and the doctors in medical school. So who would start up such a bizarre and apparently redundant activity?

Actually, quite a number of people and for various reasons. There are cultural and military historians looking for insight into how things were done in the past, looking for a truly historical martial art. There are also martial artists who find the European perspective a refreshing change after training in the Asian ways. And we get the sword lovers: people who have always just been drawn to the long, shiny, poem in steel that is a good sword. Most students who progress beyond the beginner's course have a blend of these interests, and the resurgence of western martial arts is drawing in the thugs, hippies, competitors and thespians previously mentioned. The point is that, properly taught, western swordsmanship has much to offer all the above.

There is no generally recognised regulatory body for Western martial arts. Such a body would be a practical impossibility, as it would have to arbitrate on too many conflicting fields: the martial aspect, the historical accuracy (or otherwise), etc. And there is no way to infallibly establish who would win in a real duel. A thug with a blunt sword is a dangerous animal: if you fence according to safe, reasonable, standards, you will get hammered.[6] The only reliable way to make sure that the match is an accurate simulation of reality is for the weapons to be sharp and the match fought to the death or incapacity of one or both of the fencers. This is obviously impractical. So, by and large, it is left up to the student to be able to identify those groups with a valid approach, and those without.

There are many different, more or less valid, emphases. Some instructors work mostly on the historical accuracy (which some find pedantic and dull), some are more interested in the general martial arts approach (which is prone to invalid borrowings of technical and tactical ideas from other systems), and some just offer a totally sportive interpretation. A very few schools offer training in a living tradition of Western swordsmanship, which has the authority of lineage behind it, but not everyone can travel across the world to train. Besides, the living tradition does not include any weapon earlier than the rapier. Many instructors offer as their authority the treatises written by historical masters. This has its own problems, as they are notoriously difficult to interpret, and generally written by and for advanced swordsmen. There was also little regulation in the past, so some of the treatises offer a style that may be best suited for the salle[7] or the street; some also do not clearly distinguish between training methods or weapons and those suited for combat.

The purpose of this book is to give the reader a sound theoretical and technical basis for beginning their own training, to help them establish a proper balance between the five poles, and to give them some idea of what they want from their training and how they should set about getting it. Reading this book will make absolutely no difference to your level of skill. Diligent practice of the exercises in this book will.

This book is the first volume in a proposed series that will cover basic and advanced longsword use, as well as other aspects of western martial arts. Basic longsword technique covers everything that can reasonably be made useful in a few months of intensive training. In other words, if as a medieval master at arms I had to teach a student the bare essentials of swordsmanship before sending him off to a duel, I would select a few of the exercises in this book. If he survived his duel, and decided to keep up his training, the short-term goals of this book would give way to the long-term benefits of the next, which will encapsulate the method that I teach my students at *The School of European Swordsmanship, Helsinki.*[8] This includes some remedial massage, basic nutrition and strength training, as well as the more advanced longsword techniques. Fortunately, it is highly unlikely that anyone reading this book is doing so because they are about to face an opponent holding a sharp sword wanting to kill them. Instead, you are probably interested in learning a correct method for using a longsword so that you can fence with your friends as soon as possible, and hit them more than they hit you. My students, for whom I take responsibility not only for their training, but also for their health, do not usually fence freely with a longsword until they have completed nine to twelve months of properly supervised training. The method I teach them is therefore aimed at long-term results. However, I know full well that the majority of my readers will want to freeplay[9] as soon as possible. This book, then, is designed to give you as quickly as possible the necessary groundwork for good, safe, and historically accurate longsword free fencing. That said, *I take no responsibility whatsoever for injuries you inflict or sustain due to practising the techniques in this book, or from any other source, except when you are training in my Salle or under my supervision.* Even a blunt longsword is a deadly weapon, and in any hands is extremely dangerous.

There are some groups that get around this problem by playing with padded weapons: this is all right for a fun sporting game, but does not allow the user to learn the quintessential aspect of western swordsmanship, *sentimento di ferro*[10] ("the feeling of steel," or "the sense of the blade"), which refers to the way blades interact with each other, communicated through the feeling in your hands when the blades connect. A more traditional approach includes the use of wooden weapons ("wasters") for freeplay. In the past, competitions were fought with wooden weapons and ended when one player was too badly wounded to continue, or to the first blood drawn on the head.[11] This makes you properly scared of being hit, and leads to a suitable attitude to freeplay, though is impractical in this day and age. For training purposes, wasters are certainly better than padded weapons, but still behave quite differently to a sword. At SESH we only use steel longswords, and require plastrons, fencing masks, and joint-protection during freeplay. Being hit correctly does not hurt, but my students know that with the slightest loss of attention, an accidental minor injury is possible. Combined with the proper preparatory training, this leads to excellent technical freeplay, and no injuries (to date, at least).

Questions of Attitude:
FIGHTERS, TECHNICIANS, AND SPIRITUALISTS[12]

The European tradition of swordsmanship now recognizes three distinct levels of fencing:[13] the fight, the duel, and the academy. In the fight, or at the level of the fight, the only thing that matters is to win, and quickly. This is true on the battlefield and in street defence. Because you have no idea how may opponents you actually have, nor necessarily what weapons will be involved, you must take chances. And when the penalty for losing is death or disfigurement, of course you must win at all costs.

The duel is a rather different proposition: the weapons are predetermined, the combatants know that they have only one opponent, and often some techniques were forbidden.[14] The somewhat more artificial approach of the duel allows you to carefully establish your opponent's strengths and weaknesses before committing to an attack. This allows a more technical, sophisticated, and ultimately safer style of fencing.

At the highest level of swordsmanship, the academy, there is no interest in who would actually win: the ideal is pure research, uncovering the fundamental principles of fencing. This allows the most complex and interesting swordplay. Without doubt, the best fencing I have ever had has been with masters that could take me to bits if they felt like it, but have, for the sake of mutual learning, been content to play to find out various ways of dealing with my best attacks and defences. This means that I hit them more than they would allow in a duel, but then, in the academy, that is not the point.

There are in my experience also three types of student of the sword, easily identifiable by the way they train and fence. The first and most common is the fighter. These are people who want to win, NOW. They will start freeplay as soon as they pick up a weapon, and will hone their instincts to lightning speed. They often have no discernible fear, and do very well in combat from the beginning. For them the sword is a tool, and technique that works immediately will be quickly assimilated. Most of the swordsmen I know started off like this, and this attitude is commonly encouraged in competitive martial arts (like kick-boxing), in self-defence courses, and in sport fencing.

Next, and much rarer, are the technicians. They love acquiring new techniques, and practicing them to perfection. Instinct has little to do with their fighting technique. For a couple of years, they never win a match, but after enough speed training and fencing experience, they become very good indeed. The sword is again a tool, but one for self-improvement, not winning.

Third, and rarer still are the spiritualists. These come to swordplay looking for a meditative art. The sword becomes in their hands an archetype, an ideal, an icon. They happily spend hours repeating a single cut, striving for internal and external perfection of form, and an exalted mental state akin to enlightenment. They seek and sometimes find the transcendental truth behind perfect technique. As fighters they are usually less successful to start with than their training time would indicate because they are not used to adapting to the random elements of an opponent's technique. As with the pure technicians, at first their good technique works against them because it makes them predictable. The spiritualists range from those who have a vague idea about the character-building benefits of hard training to those that practise as a form of worship to a specific deity. This attitude was actually quite well known in medieval times: some of the most feared and respected warriors belonged to knightly religious orders (the Templars are the best-known example).

We all come to the study of swordplay with one or other of these characteristics uppermost in our personality. By focusing on our strengths, we can do well quickly but will soon hit a ceiling beyond which we cannot improve. This is most obvious with the fighters, who win more and more often for a couple of years or so, and then cease to get better. The difficulty lies in developing the weaker elements. The later chapters on technique will provide the basis for a solid grounding in correct form, and I expect that most readers will look on that section as the heart of the book. In a way they are right, but the pictures and explanations are useless unless you approach them with the right attitude. Keep in mind that the art of the longsword is a means to defend yourself, a means to develop yourself, and a means to transcend yourself. Why be restricted to only one out of three? For the rarest student of all has the fighter's will to survive, the technician's enjoyment of pure technique and commitment to practice, and the spiritualist's egoless approach and deep love of the purity of form. He, or she, is truly a swordsman.

THE OBSTACLES

There are many barriers to good practice, all of them self-imposed. The first is fear of failure. What happens if you commit yourself to a course of study - mind, body, and soul- and at the end of it you aren't very good? It may seem better to just play around and have a laugh. You risk nothing. If after a few years you are still losing fights to beginners, well, you never really took it seriously, so you maybe could have beaten them if you tried as hard as they did. This attitude is very common, and takes a great deal of courage to get past.

Perhaps the most common problem that afflicts my basic-level students is a delusion of inadequacy. It is very common to see a student struggling to master a basic technique, and, after failing many times, deciding that they just aren't good enough. My normal response to this is probably infuriating for them, but it goes something like this: Do you have a duel to the death planned in the next few months? (I have never yet received a positive answer to this question.) Well, what's the hurry then? A student will commonly feel that they really should be able to do the technique already. This makes no sense; if the Art was easy, I would be unemployed. The root cause of this problem is either an initial misconception that sword-swinging must be easy because it sometimes looks easy, or an inaccurate notion of the student's own talent. This delusion is discouraging, but not usually dangerous.

Far more problematic is the delusion of adequacy. The student who thinks they already know how to do it is blind to the differences between what I am showing them and what they think I am showing them. Or worse, the student that is so certain of their own expertise that they show off by going too fast, attempting techniques that they can't control. These have to be jumped on before they hurt someone.

An accurate self-image is extremely rare. Almost everyone errs one way or another. The irony is, though, that every student I have ever had has had the intelligence and physical ability to become an expert swordsman. The only difference between my senior students and those that never made it past the beginner's course is the attitude they take to training. One the one hand, be humble enough to be really receptive to learning new things: on the other, know for certain that you are good enough to get there in the end. Hours spent practising will pay off in the long run, however many mistakes you make, and however difficult you may find the exercises. Some will find it easier than others, but everyone who trains diligently can become proficient. A martial arts instructor I trained with, John Tosney, once told me that in his experience, the harder a student finds it in the beginning, the better instructor they are likely to become: having made all the mistakes themselves, they know a dozen ways to fix them. So, frustration at the speed of your progress is a waste of emotional energy: enjoy the training, expect it to take a very long time, and before you realise it, you will become better than you ever imagined was possible.

No matter how much you train or commit yourself to the art of swordsmanship, most of us have to accept that we are not always going to win our bouts. The secret, for me, is a twofold approach. Firstly, accept that there is no end to the study of swordsmanship. There is never a point where you must pass an exam to validate yourself. You will never reach a point beyond which you cannot improve. Secondly, accept that you will never be unbeatable. There will always be at least one person who can beat you, one person who is in some way more skilled than you. So accept that you are not perfect, and move on. You undertake this study to better yourself, not to best anyone else. Indeed, at its highest level, swordsmen don't bother to count touches. I invariably learn more from fencing with superior swordsmen than from taking on easy victories.

Another common barrier is frustration. When one can see the goal ahead but just can't get the bloody thing to go where you want it, it is easy to move on to something you can already do, and practice that. Much more satisfying, and it looks better too. However, deep inside you will know that you have failed to control the weapon and, more importantly, failed to control yourself. There are three ways I use to get round this. Firstly, do not attempt the impossible, just the difficult. When the difficult has become easy, the impossible is just difficult. Set your goals just outside your limits and do not expect to get there immediately. Secondly, make a virtue out of pure practice. In other words, convince yourself that if you can already do it, it was obviously easy and so not worth bothering with again. Thirdly, go back to first principles. Establish control of your feet, legs, etc., and go through the troublesome technique at minimum speed. Increase your speed until you get it right most of the time, *however slow that may be*, and do not speed up until your skill increases to match. Believe, as a matter of faith if you will, that an hour spent trying to get something difficult right and failing, is better than that hour spent doing something that's already easy and succeeding. Trust me on this, if on nothing else.

Pride is for many the single most difficult barrier to overcome. Everyone wants to impress others. Everyone wants to feel that they are really good at what they do. And everyone wants to win their fights. The irony of this situation is that to truly achieve all these things you have to give them up. Practice for yourself, not for the spectators, and you will look better. Recognise your weaknesses and work on them, and you will become truly competent. Fight to learn, not to win, and soon enough, most people will be unable to beat you.

Why Use a Sword?

The sword is not, and never has been, the most effective weapon available. Nowadays, the gun is a far more efficient means of dispatching your enemies. But the sword is still carried in the dress uniform of almost every army in the world. Even when the sword was a functional battlefield and street-defence weapon, it was never the best. An archer could kill from further away. A well-formed block of pikemen could butcher sword-wielding men-at-arms. War-hammers, maces, and axes all pose a more direct and easily effected threat to a knight. George Silver, author of the most famous English treatise, reckoned staff weapons to be the best for single combat. The sword can cut, by focusing the energy of the blow on the smallest feasible area. Axes do that better. The sword is versatile, allowing a huge variety of techniques, counters and recounters. But so is the quarterstaff. That said, the sword does have one advantage over all others: it is the most versatile weapon that can be easily carried. A quarterstaff is too long to be really useful in a crowded tavern, and cannot be slung from a belt. The axe also needs room to swing, and has little defensive capability. A sword's thrusts or slices are still effective in a confined space, and given room to manoeuvre, it can deliver very powerful blows. The sword is small enough to carry on a belt, it can be drawn very fast, and it can, in the right hands, be used to deal with almost any defensive situation. It was not until the development of reliable, portable firearms that the sword fell into disuse.

The sword was also the most expensive weapon. The time, skill and materials needed to make a good sword meant that it would be well beond the means of the average person. Swords throughout history have been more lavishly decorated than any other class of weapon. There are extant rapier hilts, for example, that are so encrusted with gems, and made from such precious metals, that they are closer to jewellery than weaponry. The sword has always been a status symbol. As the late Ewart Oakeshott put it:

> Of all the weapons devised by Man in the long lapse of the centuries, the sword is the only one which combines effectiveness in defence with force in attack, and since its Bronze Age beginnings has gathered round itself a potent mystique which sets it above any other man-made object.[15]

As Oakeshott suggests, there is more to the sword than practicality and status symbols. In all cultures the sword has been the epitome of the Warrior archetype. Oaths have been sworn on swords. A man would be knighted by the tap of a sword on his shoulder,[16] and the soul of the samurai lay in his katana. As is shown by its symbolic use worldwide, the sword may represent honour, truth, justice, power, strength, protection.[17] It is still used in countless civil and military ceremonies, long after its battlefield usefulness has been superceded. Most people who take up the study of swordsmanship instinctively grin when they heft a sword in their hand. The sword's enduring position in human culture speaks for my (finally unverifiable) view that somehow the sword speaks to the soul in a way no other weapon ever has. It focuses the physical, mental and spiritual energy of the swordsman in a way no other weapon can. The sword is the ultimate weapon of transcendence.

"In Life as in Fence, in Fence as in Life"

There are many levels at which you can enjoy the study of swordsmanship. It can be an academic interest, an amusing hobby, a fitness programme, even a profession. It does not have to be deliberately chosen as a lifestyle. Personally, I practised for ten years before coming to the realisation that my practice did not get left behind when I hung up my weapon. It stays with you in the way you move, in how you arrange your time, and in how you deal with people. The principles of tactics and strategy learned in training underpin the way I deal with confrontation at any level. But most importantly, the practice crystallises your approach to life in general. It becomes a testing ground for character: it holds up a mirror that can not be ignored. It exposes every flaw, every weakness *and thereby allows you to overcome them*. It will never expose a problem to which there is no solution. It teaches, above all, that you can work on your weaknesses and develop your strengths. The sword cannot lie to you. Listening to it often hurts. But there is *always* a way through.

ChAPTER 2
The WEAPON

A Brief History of the Longsword

As Sir Richard Burton begins his masterly *Book of the Sword* "the history of the sword is the history of humanity."[1] Since man first picked up a rock and bashed someone's head in, he has been developing new and interesting tools for accomplishing the same end. The earliest swords were probably charred bits of wood good only for thrusting. Sticks with flints attached to create a long cutting edge were probably next, then with the discovery of metal came longish copper knives. Copper was later mixed with tin to make bronze, so knives could be made even longer without them folding up embarrassingly at the worst possible moment.

Obviously, as the metals available became stronger, longer blades could be made light enough to wield, thus giving their owner a reach advantage without slowing them down too much. Most knightly weapons up to the advent of plate armour were designed to be used one-handed with a shield. As armour improved, the weapons changed to penetrate it, and at the same time, knights could afford to trust their armour and use a two-handed weapon.

Choosing any armour/weapon combination has always been a compromise between mobility and protection, reach and manoeuverability, offensive and defensive capabilities. Full plate armour was developed by the late-fourteenth century, and knights would practice and joust in armour that would normally weigh about 55 pounds.[2] Using sharp swords or heavy pole-arms, they would batter away at each other for the agreed number of blows, either just to prove their valour, or to settle a grievance. On campaign they may have had to fight all day, march or ride the next, then fight again. So generally speaking, knights would go into battle in a harness of plate in which they would be able to run, jump, roll, kick, and swing a sword with ease. The modern myth about knights in inch-thick steel plate being winched onto cart-horses is an over-literal interpretation of the hyperbole of medieval poetry, accompanied by a modern confusion between jousting, tourney armour, and the armour worn into battle.[3] No knight was ever winched onto his horse.

For men-at-arms who favoured the sword over the axe, the pole-arm or the mace, there developed a weapon that compromised between the reach of a two-handed weapon (such as a poleaxe), and the manoeuverability of the single-hander; yet light enough to allow the use of a secondary defensive arm, such as a buckler, a shield or a dagger. This paragon of the late medieval/early renaissance era was the longsword.

So, What Is a Longsword?

Sword types tend to blend into each other: when does an arming sword[4] become a longsword or a greatsword or a two-handed sword? For convenience, I prefer to define them by the the length of their handles. An arming sword's handle can only comfortably fit one hand; a longsword can fit two, but the weapon is light enough and the handle short enough, to be wielded with one hand (a very long handle gets in the way if your other hand is not on it), and a two-handed sword has a handle and mass that clearly requires both hands. A greatsword is basically a large longsword or a small two-hander, about the equivalent of the fifteenth-century English term "longsword." As a guideline: when holding the sword in your hand at the crossguard, if the pommel can touch your wrist, it's an arming sword; above the wrist and below the elbow it's a longsword; at the elbow or above, it's a two-hander. This is not a technical definition, but a sword-user's rule of thumb. The techniques in this book are designed for a weapon that fits this definition of "longsword."

In fifteenth-century English "longsword" referred to a two-handed sword. What we call a longsword today was, in English up until quite recently (late twentieth-century), usually called a hand-and-a-half sword, or a bastard sword. The term "longsword" in modern usage is a translation of the German *Langes Schwert* from the German *Fechtbücher* that deal with, among other weapons, the hand-and-a-half sword, and from the Italian *spadone* from Vadi's *De Arte Gladiatoria Dimicandi* (circa 1482-1487)[5] and Fiore's *Flos Duellatorum* (1409). By and large, what we know about the use of the longsword comes from treatises written in Italy and Germany, though it was certainly popular elsewhere.[6] What few English treatises we have that cover this weapon[7] usually refer to it as a "two-hand sword". They are far less comprehensive and accessible than the German and Italian treatises, so perhaps for this reason the historical swordplay community has, by and large, adopted the direct translation of the German term. For convenience I shall follow this convention.

Longswords came in a huge range of styles, categorised in eight distinct types by the late Ewart Oakeshott.[8] They could be designed primarily for cutting, with parallel edges (such as type XIIIa), or for thrusting, with edges that taper (such as type XVa). They could weigh as little as two pounds (0.91kg) or as much as four (1.82kg),[9] and the point of balance could range from the cross-guard to half-way down the blade, though was most commonly about three inches (75mm) from the cross-guard. Pages 158 and 160 of *Records of the Medieval Sword* show examples of otherwise very similar weapons that handle completely differently; according to Oakeshott, one is "surprisingly light and

Figure 2.1: *The weapon illustrated in Fillipo Vadi's 15th century work,* Di Arte Gladiatoria Dimicandi, *for use against an armoured opponent.*

responsive in the hand, weighing just over 2 lbs, [the other] is heavy, even clumsy - a sort of bar of iron ... needing a lot of strength to use" (p. 157). He goes on to remark that the latter weighs "nearly four pounds ... the point of balance nearly half-way to the point" (p. 160).

As a civilian[10] side-arm, the longsword had many advantages. It was the longest weapon that could reasonably be worn at the hip.[11] Indeed, the ideal length for your longsword is the longest one that you can draw in one movement from a belt-slung scabbard. This gives you the maximum reach for your point, and the maximum tip-speed for your cuts[12] (this will be discussed at length in the technique section). The sword being primarily used with two hands, and manoeuverable enough for a strong defence, there was no need to carry a shield or buckler. The beauty of this weapon is that being light enough for single-handed use, the left arm was available for disarms, locks and throws. As you will see in the relevant chapters, many longsword techniques involve closing in and grappling with the left hand.

The development of defensive rings on the hilts of longswords suggest that it was quite common practice to hook the forefinger of your sword hand over the crossguard to improve the heft of the weapon by shifting the grip closer to the point of balance, and also to prevent the sword turning in your grip.[13] This habit naturally exposed that finger to the risk of being broken or severed by a blow running down the blade, and so a ring would sometimes be attached to the cross to protect the finger (see Oakeshott p.204 for an example). The historical record of sword hilts shows that over time, more rings were added, affording greater protection to the hand (see Oakeshott p.241). During this process, the blade of the civilian side-arm got lighter and faster to use until there was no further need to have two hands on the hilt.

Towards the end of the fifteenth century the *spada da lato* ("sidesword") had developed from the "civilian" longsword (while you are looking up the previous Oakeshott references, by all means have a look at pages 242 and 243 for examples). This weapon has been called a cut-and-thrust sword, a sword-rapier, or even a rapier.[14] The process of the civilian sidearm getting lighter and faster continued until in the late seventeenth-century it culminated in the last of the fencing sidearms, the smallsword.[15]

The "military" longsword was another matter entirely. The circumstances of battle meant that there would be little room to manoeuvre, opponents would often be armoured, and the combatant would be facing heavy weapons like poleaxes, axes and maces. So the blade had to be heavier in order to withstand parrying heavier weapons, and to make an impact through armour. Different techniques had to be employed: a raking slice across the belly may finish an unarmoured duel, but will just blunt your sword against a breastplate. Against armour, the thrust is the preferred attack, as the point can be effectively wedged between plates and into vulnerable joints. The armoured combat sections of both Fiore and Vadi's treatises show the point used for this purpose, and Vadi goes so far as to recommend a significantly different weapon, the *spada in arme*, which looks much like a longsword but is designed to be used primarily with one hand on the hilt and the other three-quarters of the way up the blade.

On the first page of the Getty manuscript of Fiore's treatise there is a picture of a similar weapon, and in the Pisani Dossi, he shows one guard with an apparently similar weapon, probably used for hunting boar (see illustration 2.2 below).

The longsword was probably the first sword designed primarily to be enough on its own. All previous sword types, from the gladius through the Viking sword and including the European single-handed sword, were generally used with a shield or buckler. Early treatises for the single-hander, (such as Royal Armouries Manuscript I.33, from about 1295) emphasise the use of a secondary weapon, like a buckler,[16] so the longsword was probably the first sword for which a complete system of fence was developed in Europe for the sword alone.

Figure 2.2: *Fiore dei Liberi's illustration for a similar weapon shown in Fillipo Vadi's treatise (fig. 2.1 facing page). From the Pisani-Dossi Fiore dei Liberi, carta 17B, fig. 6.*

ChAPTER 3
The Italian Masters
Fiore dei Liberi and Filippo Vadi[1]

I f you want to know the best way to use any tool, ask a professional, one whose life and livelihood depends on his skill. The sword is no exception. Fortunately, the professional swordsmen of the past did occasionally write down their methods. These manuscripts[2] were generally written for a patron, and often illustrated to show the techniques in some detail. As always, the gap between practical technique and its verbal and pictorial representation is difficult to bridge. One of the main purposes of this book is to narrow the gap, with more detailed explanations of exactly how each technique is done, using modern English (early Italian is almost as hard to interpret as medieval handwriting), with clear, accurate illustrations.

There are two major historical styles of longsword use; Italian and German. Both have their merits, both are correct. My preference is for the Italian. The core treatises for my method of longsword are Fiore dei Liberi's *Flos Duellatorum* (written in 1409),[3] and Filippo Vadi's *De Arte Gladiatoria Dimicandi* (written between 1482 and 1487) . Hidden behind the text and hinted at in the pictures lies the quintessentially Latin flavour of Italian swordsmanship. Though Italy as a unified political entity was four hundred years in the future, the Italian style, which would culminate in Ferrari and Armani, breathes life into the pages of these long-forgotten treatises. These treatises are not just collections of blocks, strikes, binds and throws; they each describe a way of approaching combat, a way of moving, a separate body-language. It is the feeling for this essence (in any fencing style of any nationality) that for me marks the truly historical swordsman.

Fiore and Vadi speak different dialects of this language: I see Vadi as more engaged in turning motions, Fiore's style as more linear. But the energy behind the moves is identifiably similar. There is a strong case to be made for taking each master separately, for pointing out the differences in their methods, showing up each style's strengths and weaknesses. However, there are two main problems with this, deriving from the fact the treatises were written for other masters or advanced students. Firstly, the masters largely left out the really basic information, such as exactly how to execute a cut correctly. Secondly, they present in their treatises their own *emphasis*, their own idiosyncratic ideas of the "best" moves and their own personal style. Fiore acknowledges the "excellent masters, Italian and foreign" that taught him, yet presents a synthesis of his knowledge, not the fragments. Once you have mastered the basics, and have a thorough grounding in the eternal and fundamental principles of swordsmanship, it will be up to you to see which parts of Vadi's system suit you best, which of Fiore's techniques work against which opponents. Every move in these treatises is effective: I have used most in freeplay at some time or another. With time and practice, your own style will develop, just as it would have had you been learning this weapon in earnest 550 years ago. Provided you are using the right techniques *in the right way*, you will be using a thoroughly authentic fifteenth-century Italian style. So the technical section represents a synthesis based on research into the techniques of Fiore and Vadi. I believe that you can do well to be, like Fiore, taught by many masters, to have as many different approaches, moves and counters in your arsenal as possible.

For the purposes of gleaning theoretical principles, the most important parts of these treatises are the pages, reproduced below, describing the underlying ideas of the systems with symbols and text. Interpreting the symbols precisely is no easy matter, and the context of the time must be taken into account. However, by taking a good look at the various animals and other symbols depicted in these pages, the main points of Fiore's and Vadi's systems become clear.

What follows is by no means an in-depth survey of the possible nuances of symbolic significance that may be derived from these images. That would take a book in itself. I have confined myself to covering the main interpretations, useful to a beginner swordsman, and suggesting further avenues of enquiry for those particularly interested in this aspect of the subject. [4]

FLOS DUELLATORUM (1409)

The basis of Fiore's swordsmanship principles are found in the four animals, shown on this page, known as the "Seven Swords". The animal on the left is a tiger (*tígro*), holding an arrow. This represents the quality of *celeritas*, meaning swiftness. At the top there is a lynx (*louo ceruino*),[5] holding a pair of compasses. He represents *prudentia* (prudence). The lion (*lione*) on the right, with his paw on a heart, represents *audatia*, boldness or courage. The elephant (*Ellefât*), below, represents *fortitudo*, strength. The positioning of these animals around the man is highly significant, as are the symbols each one carries.[6]

The Segno of Fiore dei Liberi

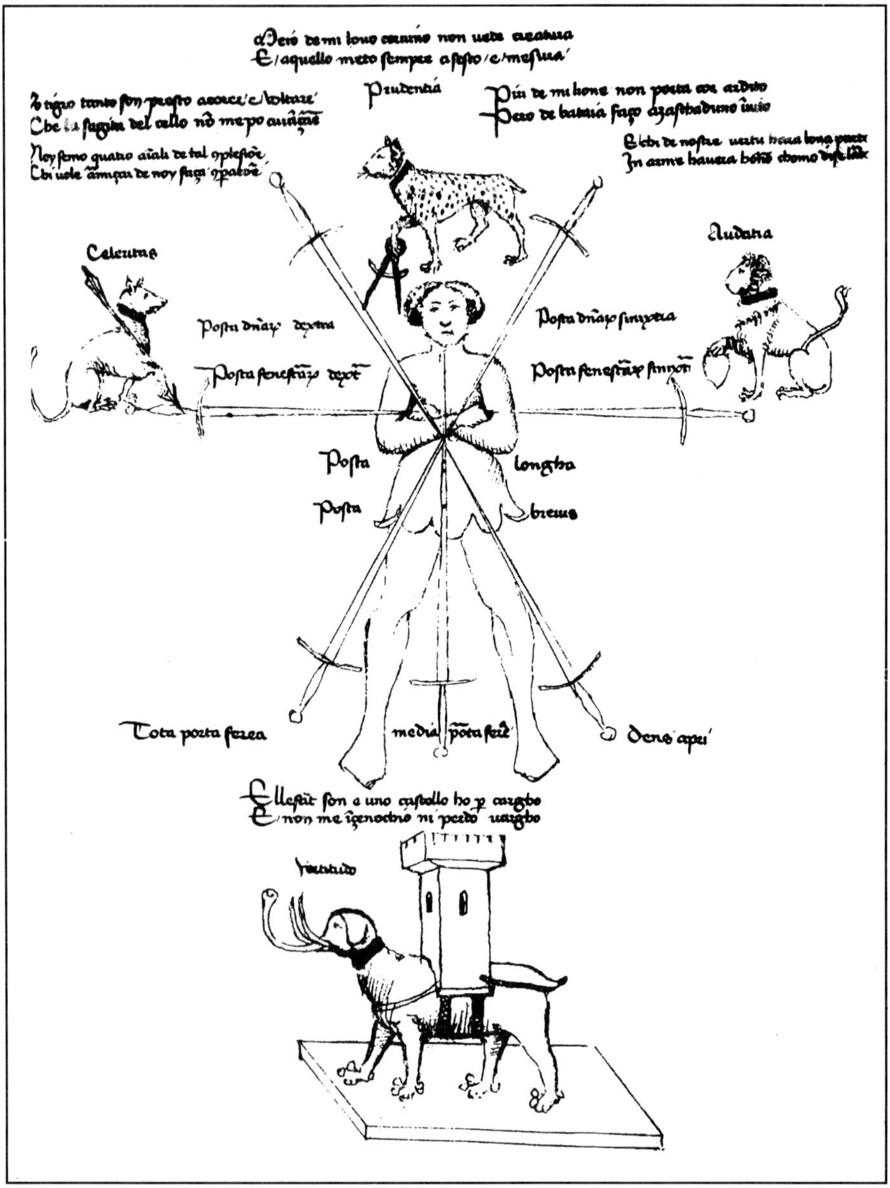

Figure 3.1: *The "segno" illustration of Fiore dei Liberi, from the Pisani-Dossi edition. The illustrations, symbolic representations of different fighting aspects, are core components of the Italian fighting tradition as it survives.*

The Lynx

The Lynx is situated over the head, and carries a pair of dividers. The text with it translates as:

> **Prudentia**/Prudence[7]
>
> *No other creature can see clearer than I, the Lynx,*
> *Who always brings posture and measure.*[8]

The dividers, or compasses, are a common symbol of precise judgement and careful measurement. Necessary in geometry, the most advanced branch of mathematics at that time, they are easily recognisable as the symbol of the thinker, the creator, and the scientist.[9] It is no coincidence that the first modern scientific academy, founded in Rome in 1603 by Frederico Cesi, was called the Academy of the Linceans, alluding to "Lyncaeus, the most keen-eyed of the Argonauts, and to the lynx, credited with the most acute vision in the animal kingdom."[10] In combination, the Lynx and the dividers embody the principle of precise, careful judgement of distance and time leading to victory in combat.

In the Getty manuscript, the Lynx represents *avisamento*, (in modern Italian, *avvisamento*) which best translates as 'foresight', and implies prophecy. The Lynx and the dividers are there to remind the student to be prudent, to carefully judge distance and time, and to learn to predict the actions of his opponent.

The Elephant

> **Fortitudo**/Strength
>
> *I am the Elephant and have a castle for a load.*
> *I do not fall on my knees, nor miss my step.*

The association of elephants with strength is an obvious one, and the tower in the illustration is made to look like a castle, also a symbol of strength. Positioned at the man's feet, it is the only animal of the four to be standing on a stable, level surface, emphasising the importance of terrain and footwork. A counterbalance to mental strength, the elephant represents bodily strength, which is derived from a strong connection to the ground and correct body mechanics.

The strength of the structure derives from two things: the elephant's physical strength, and his balance. However strong the elephant may be, if the tower does not stay upright, he will fall. In this period the elephant was widely believed to have no knees: hence if he falls down, he cannot rise, and he cannot kneel at all. As in *Flos Duellatorum*, bestiary elephants are often depicted with battle-towers ("howdahs") on their back.

The elephant represents the swordsman's legs, supporting the torso, represented by the tower. To be strong, keep your back straight, your legs firm, and your feet on stable ground.

The Tiger

The word "tiger" actually derives from the ancient Persian word for arrow. In the bestiary tradition, tigers are usually spotted, never striped, and were principally associated with speed. They are also variously drawn like a dog (as in *Flos Duellatorum*), or a horse, presumably because those animals are also known to be swift.

Celeritas/Swiftness

I, the Tiger, am quick at running and dodging
That the arrow[11] in the sky cannot overtake me.

The tiger in the picture is holding an arrow, confirming the traditional and linguistic link. He is sitting by the right shoulder of the man, which suggests that it is the speed of the right hand (or sword-arm) that is most crucial.[12] The arrow is not only fast, it is also accurate. With a fifteenth-century hunting longbow, a good archer should be able to place three arrows into a two-inch circle at forty yards. Traditional archers of my acquaintance can do even better. Both the tiger and the arrow are fast and deadly. So the principle of Swiftness here is not just speed, but speed allied to accuracy and focus.

The Lion

The lion is traditionally the King of Beasts, and has symbolised courage since time immemorial. (King Richard the Lionheart was called so because of his courage in battle. Even the lion in *The Wizard of Oz* was looking for courage!), and it is present on many coats-of-arms. Its main allegorical significance in the bestiaries is the representation of various attributes of Christ. Fiore's lion is pugnacious:

Audatia/Boldness

None has a bolder heart than I, the Lion,
And I challenge everyone to battle.

Fiore is calling on his students to be bold, to be willing to fight. There are two reasons for this. Firstly, fifteenth-century Italy was a dangerous place. There was constant factional infighting, and it was part of Fiore's job to prepare the subjects of his patron, Niccolo, Marquis of Ferrara, Modena, Parma and Reggio, to fight on the Marquis' behalf. Secondly, and more importantly for modern students of the sword, it is vital to let go of fear of injury: to face opponents bravely. The reason for this is practical: if you are terrified of getting hurt, you do everything possible to minimise the short-term likelihood of pain, and just instinctively block the attacks. Taken too far, this fear can prevent you from hitting back at all - in which case getting hit yourself is just a matter of time. It takes a huge amount of focused intention to counterattack: it is a bit like jumping out of an aeroplane. You have to *know* your counter will work, just as you have to *know* your parachute will open. That is the principle of *audatia* here: overcome your natural fear with the belief that you *will* succeed. The Lion stands his ground audaciously against any opponent. At the end of the treatise, Fiore reiterates:

> *Be audacious in the attack and let your soul not be old*
> *Have no fear in your mind; be on guard, you can make it.*
> *Take the woman for an example, fearful and stricken by panic, she*
> *would never face the naked steel.*
> *And so a fearful man is worth less than a woman. If you don't have*
> *audacity of heart, all else is missing.*
> *Audacity, such virtue is what this art is all about.*

Despite his dated notions regarding women as fencers, nevertheless, Fiore's emphasis on boldness as the main virtue of the swordsman is interesting, and should be taken to heart by the modern student of the sword.

The Four in One
The text goes on to say:

> *We are four animals with these traits.*
> *He who wants to battle should measure with us.*
> *And he who has a good portion of our virtues,*
> *He will have honour in battle, according to the art.*

The message here, as in most philosophies, is that balance is all. The virtues symbolised by these animals are useless on their own. Prudence is nothing without the Boldness to fight, the Swiftness to fight well, and the Strength to make your actions work. Take away any of these qualities, and you will lose. Exaggerate any one beyond reason, and you will lose. Achieve a harmonious blend of all four, and you may overcome.

The Lion and the Tiger are balanced across the chest of the swordsman: he must be bold enough to stand, focused and determined enough to attack swiftly. And he must be balanced by a strong, grounded body that will execute the commands of a clear, prudent head.

The Signo of Fillipo Vadi

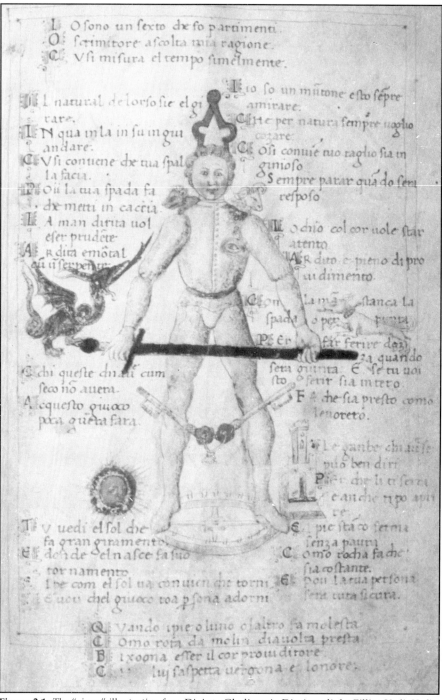

Figure 3.1: *The "signo" illustration from* Di Arte Gladiatoria Dimicandi, *by Fillipo Vadi. Vadi includes a separate cutting diagram, but expands on the number and complexity of the symbols he uses to communicate his fighting philosophy. Photo courtesy the Biblioteca Nazionale, Rome.*

De Arte Gladiatoria Dimicandi (1482-1487)

The principles of Vadi's system are similar in many ways to Fiore's. However, Vadi has a different approach, and he emphasises the different uses of body parts more clearly than Fiore, using some different animals to illustrate his ideas. Taken in turn, each part of the body is illustrated with a symbol that describes its proper function.

The head is the seat of judgement, represented by the **dividers** (*sexto*), as in Fiore. The accompanying text reads:

> Oh, I am the compass, which divides.
> Oh swordsman, listen to my reasoning;
> Match rhythm[13] and timing together.[14]

This is a simple admonition to the student to be precise in the judgement of timing and distance. Don't lose your head or you will lose your head!

> At the right[15] shoulder is a **bear** (*orso*).[16]
> The nature of the Bear is to turn.
> Here and there, up and down.
> Thus your shoulder must move.
> So your sword may hunt.

In this way, your shoulder should roam around, looking for openings, prowling after your opponent like a bear in the woods. The right hand is characterised as a **dragon** (*serpente*).

> The right hand must be prudent
> Bold and deadly like a dragon.

Traditionally, the dragon is "the greatest of all serpents ... its strength is not in its teeth, but its tail, which harms by lashing" (MacCullough, p. 112). The dragon is facing up the arm, with the head level with the elbow. As I see it, this suggests that the elbow is the head of the dragon (this makes sense as close-quarters techniques to the elbow are usually more immediately incapacitating than those to the hand or shoulder), the hand is the body of the dragon, and the sword its tail (which hurts by "lashing").

On the left shoulder is a **ram** (*mūtone*), for barging your opponent when at close quarters:

> I am a Ram, always looking for an opening,
> Whose nature to butt.
> So your cut should be ingenious
> And always parry when there is a riposte.

Ramming with the left shoulder is a part of many of the *giocco stretto* (close quarters) techniques I will be describing later. Perhaps even more important, though, is the idea of always being ready to parry when attacking. It will be emphasised later that you should never attack without thought of defence; so your attacks should be "ingenious".

The **greyhound** (*leuoreto*)[17] is at the left hand.

> The left hand on the sword is for the point
> To make it strike when it arrives
> And if you want to make it complete
> Make it as swift as the hound.

The text refers to the left hand as controlling the point, this gives you the stability, strength and speed to thrust accurately and hard. The close-quarter grapples will also require your left hand to hunt like a hound, seeking out its target with devastating speed. The greyhound attacks by catching its prey in its mouth; so your left hand will find targets to grip.

The **eye** (*ochio*) on the left side of the body indicates that your awareness of your opponent should not come from your vision alone. The text is enigmatic:

> The eye of the heart must stay alert
> Bold and full of providence.

In other words, you must use your vision and your instinct when fencing. Vadi is probably hinting here at the kind of sixth sense swordsmen develop over many years of training. This symbol also suggests to me that when fencing you should not stare at your opponent's face or sword but look through him. In practice, this allows you to use your scotopic vision (using the retinal rod cells), which is much faster and more sensitive to movement than your photopic vision (using the retinal cone cells). Once the eye focusses on one spot, your ability to sense movement is reduced. Boldness[18] and the judgement of measure (or distance) are key virtues in Vadi's sytem, as in Fiore's.

There is a saying common among sportsmen: "You're only as good as your knees." Vadi makes this point clearly, by placing a pair of **keys** (*chiaū*) at the knees of the swordsman.

> And he who has not these keys with him
> In this play will make little war
> The legs could well be called keys
> Because they close and also they can open.[19]

Vadi instructs his readers not to lumber along, but step smoothly, bending the legs. It is common to see beginners walking stiff-legged, hiking their hips up and down. As Vadi suggests, bending the knees is the first step towards more graceful, fluid motion.

The feet are depicted with the **Sun** (*sol*) and a **tower** (unnamed), on a **millwheel** (*rota da molin*). The texts read:

> You see the sun that makes great turns
> And he returns where he is born
> The foot like the sun should come back
> If you want your person to be adorned by
>   the play…
> The left foot without fear is still
> Be sure it is as stable as a rock
> And then your whole person will be sure…
> When one or the other foot becomes a
>   hindrance
> Like a mill wheel they should quickly turn
> The heart should provide for that
> (As it's) up to him the shame and honor[20]

In the fifteenth century, it was generally accepted that the Sun moved around the Earth in a circular orbit. So the Sun at the right foot describes the motion of that foot: moving circularly around the tower of the left foot. As with the tower on the elephant's back in Fiore's work, the tower represents strength. Obviously, you must move both feet when fighting: the text is telling us to keep one foot firmly planted at all times, to move fluidly, in a circular stepping motion. In other words, this is a system for getting us to the right place, at the right time, in balance. In the footwork exercises later in this book, I will emphasise again the importance of keeping your knees bent, and maintaining a solid connection to the ground; principles represented here by the keys and the tower.

Now that we have had a look at these pages from the treatises, how can the insights from them be applied? Fiore's four principles form the structure of the training method I have developed, the basics of which are detailed in this book. First comes body mechanics, and the correct physical execution of techniques. Then we work on the ability to boldly execute those techniques against an attack. With practice, the techniques can be applied swiftly and accurately. Regular training with strong, swift, accurate techniques leads to an understanding of distance and timing. Strength matched with swiftness, boldness with prudence, and an emphasis on counterattacking, forms the core of my longsword method. Vadi is more specific about how to go about obtaining each quality, and adds details of the body mechanics and close-quarter tactics that we use in practice.

These pages are among the earliest fencing sources that we have, but they clearly show a properly thought-out system of training that no doubt paved the way for the more complex developments of fencing theory. From them, and from other works, it is possible to synthesise a clear and comprehensive system of physical practice and an intellectual understanding of that practice. First it is necessary to clarify for the beginner some of the terminology and theoretical principles that will be relied upon later, but have not been covered in this section.

CHAPTER 4
FENCING PRINCIPLES[1]

encing principles govern fencing actions. Fully understanding them can only come from diligent practice of the techniques, but that practice will be more efficient if you can use the principles to analyse the particular action you are working on. If it is not working properly, applying the principles can really help you figure out where it is going wrong. As we saw in the previous chapter, fencing principles as defined by Fiore and Vadi mainly refer to the qualities of the swordsman, and his body-mechanics, rather than providing a clear method for analysing the individual techniques.

My experience as a martial artist, fencer and instructor has led me to define techniques according to the following criteria. (This is my own way of conceptualizing techniques, not a part of general or historical fencing theory as far as I am aware.) As I see it, all techniques are specific to distance, timing, configuration and direction. These four principles are interdependent, they each affect the others. For a technique to work, all four aspects must be correct.

1. **Distance**: any given technique will usually work at only one distance. A cut that misses by a millimetre still misses. For example, at close quarters (*giocco stretto*), a push to the elbow does nothing against the forearm, and nothing against the shoulder, but applied to the exact location of the elbow joint, can easily destroy your opponent's balance. As distance is the clearest distinction, the one most convenient to illustrate and most obvious for a beginner to be able to distinguish, all the techniques in this book are divided up first and foremost by the distances at which they work. You must also be able to judge the distances at which you are safe from your opponent's actions to avoid them successfully.

2. **Timing**: there is a window of opportunity that is open for a finite time (usually a fraction of a second) in which it is possible to execute a given technique successfully. Timing is perhaps the most controversial, awkward to describe, and most sophisticated aspect of fencing.

3. **Configuration**: which bit goes where? Configuration refers to the relative shapes in which your opponent's body and yours are at the time of the technique. In other words, is his arm bent or straight? Which side is forward? Which hand are you in a position to use, and exactly how will it relate to its target? Obviously, the elbow push mentioned above will not work if his arm is not extended, for example. Configuration tends to be the most obvious difficulty faced by a beginner, who will generally need to have the exact mechanics of each technique explained. I have tried to do this in the technical exercises.

4. **Direction**: this describes the relative vectors of your momenta. In other words, where is he going, along what line, and how does that intersect with your own direction of movement? Is his weight moving in a linear or circular fashion? Along the line of direction (the straight line between two fencers facing each other) or at a diagonal? And how are you moving? Against a static opponent, you can only strike: it is usually impossible to apply locks, limb-destructions or throws against someone who is standing still. (Abnormal differences in strength, or passivity on the part of your opponent change this, of course.) Most *giocco stretto* techniques, for example, require you to use your opponent's momentum to apply the force.

So you must be in the right place, going the right way, at the right time to use a technique specific to that particular distance, time, configuration and direction. Not as hard as it sounds, as the technical exercises will hopefully make clear.

Configuration and direction will be covered by the techniques chapters, but first a word on distance and timing. As emphasised by Fiore and Vadi, and all other fencing masters that I have come across on the page or in the flesh, accurate judgement of distance and timing is one of the most important skills a swordsman must learn. Timing and distance are two sides of one coin; they exist relative to each other and dependent on each other. A step may be taken to change the distance to create the time in which to strike. The fencing principles outlined below are specific to the longsword, though are in part applicable to other weapons as well.

DISTANCE

Fiore divides longsword fencing into two types: *giocco largo* (long play) and *giocco stretto* (close play). These terms refer to the type of fencing that is done (the "play") not to the distance itself, so when describing the distances, I am inferring a distinction. At longer range, where there is no immediate threat from your opponent's weapon, you are outside of fencing distance.[2]

GIOCCO LARGO

Giocco largo occurs in any distance where a cut or thrust may land with one or no steps, and I subdivide it into two distances:

1. **Long range**: where with one step you can launch an attack that will land.
2. **Short range**: the distance from which an attack can be launched without stepping, for example to the hands. If the blades are engaged at this range (and they should be!), the engagement will be at the middle of the blades (*meza spada*).[3]

The distances blend into each other: at the shorter measures of long range, it may be possible to engage; when engaged closely enough, an attack may be launched without a step. Fencing distance is therefore partly a matter of physical proximity (how many inches between one fencer's chest and the other's), and partly to do with intention (for example, whether the blades are offered out for engagement). It is also possible for the distance to be different for each fencer: either due to their respective heights, reaches and lengths of blade, or due to the direction they are facing in. For example, it is possible to sidestep a long range attack, and counter-attack to the wrists, while being in a position where the first attacker is still in long range (he has to take another step to hit) while the defender is in short range (he can hit again without stepping).

GIOCCO STRETTO

You are at *giocco stretto* when you can touch your opponent with your hand. All unarmed, dagger, and hilt attacks (e.g. pommel strikes) are done at this distance. I divide *giocco stretto* into four distances:[4]

1. **Wrist-distance**: at this range, you can grab your opponent's wrist.
2. **Elbow-distance**: at this range, you can comfortably grab or push your opponent's elbow.
3. **Shoulder-distance**: at this range your shoulder is against theirs, and you can barge or throw them.
4. **Back-distance**: at this range, you are effectively behind your opponent. Techniques at this distance are usually done against the neck.

This page from *Flos Duellatorum* shows one technique in each of the four distances.

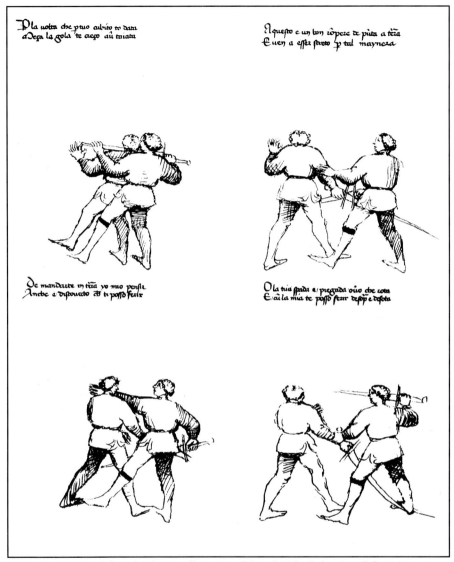

Figure 4.1: *Carta 14b from the* Flos Duellatorum *of Fiore dei Liberi, showing all four* giocco stretto *distances.*

The many *giocco stretto* techniques done in longsword fencing are usually specific to distance: you cannot execute a wrist-distance technique at shoulder-distance. The term "wrist-distance" does not necessarily imply a technique done against that part of the anatomy: there are wrist-locks that are done at shoulder-distance and one of the most common wrist-distance attacks is a pommel-strike to the face. Techniques may also combine distances: entering into wrist-distance to grab the inside of the sword-wrist, closing in to elbow-distance to lock the arm, then finishing in back-distance to break the arm and throw the opponent, all in one smooth action. The important thing to remember is that the specific action you are doing must be done at the right distance.

LINES OF ATTACK AND DEFENCE

A *line of attack* refers to the target and the trajectory the attack takes to achieve that target. The lines of attack with a longsword are clearly shown in both *Flos Duellatorum* and *De Arte Gladiatoria*. The "Seven Swords" (segno) page from the Pisani Dossi manuscript reproduced on p. 20 also determines the guards which effectively close each line.

An open line is an avenue of attack that your opponent may exploit without going through your sword. Closing a particular line means to interpose the defensive part of your weapon between your opponent's blade and the target threatened by that line. Obviously, by closing one line you necessarily open another.

The golden rule of fencing is only attack an opening line.

Of course, if your opponent is not moving, there are no opening lines: some lines are open, one is probably closed, depending on the guard adopted. So you must force him to move, creating an opening line. (A favourite trick of experienced fencers when fencing the less experienced is to subtly manoeuvre so that a line the beginner thinks is closed is actually open, then hit him with a surprise attack. In effect, by moving your position relative to your opponent, you are creating an opening line.) All blade defence relies on closing the line of your opponent's attack: all offence relies on making sure the line that you are attacking will be open when your attack arrives. Every technique in this book is designed to enable you to first perceive the lines of attack, then to open or close them at will, and finally to manipulate and exploit them. Because all lines lead to the centre, closing the line of attack closes the centre relative to that line. This is often referred to (in western and eastern martial arts) as just "closing the centre."

INSIDE/OUTSIDE

The terms *inside* and *outside* are used frequently in swordsmanship, and must be clearly understood. Usually, *inside* refers to the front of the body, and *outside* to the back. However, the reference may be to the defender, the attacker, the sword or the swordsman, depending on context.

These terms were effectively codified after the longsword period, when the weapon would always be held in one hand, and the swordsman would always lead with the same foot. In that case, for a right-handed swordsman inside and outside are simply left and right of the sword respectively. Things become a little more complex when dealing with a two-handed weapon which permits either foot to lead.

If a right-handed swordsman is on guard, right foot forwards, and the blade over on his right, then any attack to the right of his sword is *outside*. The same swordsman, in a mirror position, left foot forwards, blade on his left closing that line, changes the aspect of his body (now that same attack to his right side is coming on the inside line).

The inside and outside lines of attack are also defined as *high* or *low*. This refers only to the position of the sword: attacks above the sword are in the high line, attacks below are in the low line, wherever the sword may be.

With deflections or any other defensive action against your opponent or his

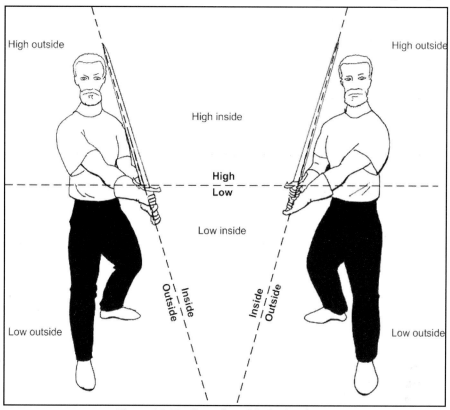

Figure 4.2: *Key lines of attack in fencing theory.*

sword, *inside* and *outside* refer to the attacker's movements. A cut coming from your left will usually be made with your opponent stepping forwards with his right foot. Thus to get to his *outside*, you must deflect the weapon up to the right, while stepping to the left. Such a deflection, done behind the attacker's cut, is an outside deflection. Another way of looking at it is to think of it as moving inside or outside the arc of the cut.

OPPOSITION

Opposition describes the situation in which the defensive part of your sword is positioned so that the direct line of your opponent's attack is closed, usually while you are attacking. To be in opposition does not necessarily require you to have blade contact, though in practice you normally do. In general, you should always fence "in opposition", so that your opponent cannot get a clean shot at you when you attack.

The principle of opposition is most easily understood in the context of a counter-attack with the point. Imagine that your opponent cuts down at your left shoulder. As he cuts, push your point into his face, while catching his cut on the blade of your sword near the hilt (this action is described in more detail in the Thrusts section, exercise three, *Vertical Opposition*). This counter-attack is safe is because you have closed the line of his attack.

You should strive to acquire opposition even when attacking. This is done by analysing your opponent's position, and working out which is his most likely line of counter-attack, then making sure that your sword closes that line as you attack, counterattack, or riposte.

TIMING

Timing is notoriously difficult to describe in words. Just as distance is only partly a matter of feet and inches, so timing is only partly about seconds and hundredths of seconds. In fencing terms, time is always relative to your and your opponent's actions. The technical terms associated with matters of timing are also partly dependent on the weapon used, and timing has been hair-splittingly defined and redefined throughout the ages. For our purposes, we need only define a few terms.

> *Fencing time*: one unit of fencing time is the time it takes to execute one fencing action. Different fencing actions will have different real-time lengths, and every fencer will have different speeds at which he can do any action.

With the longsword, there are two essential ways of timing your defence, all relative to an attack made by your opponent.

> *Due tempi* ("two-times" or "double-time"): this describes the timing of your actions when you defend before you offend. Parry-then-riposte, deflect-then-cut. Your defensive action must occur in the time of your opponent's attack, your offensive action occurs in a second unit of fencing time. However, if your two blade actions are completed withing the time of your opponents attack (which is possible because a full attack takes longer to do that a simple parry-riposte), your defence is still *due tempi*, because you are executing two movements, and therefore must use two units of fencing time. A **parry** is a block or deflection of your opponent's attack; a **riposte** is the attack immediately following a successful parry.[5]

> *Mezzo tempo* ("middle-time"): this describes the timing when one fencer makes an action in the middle of the other's, and is most commonly used in this book in reference to a **counterattack** in the time of your opponent's attack. In other words, you hit him during his attack. To be termed a counterattack, it must occur in the same unit of fencing time as the original attack.[6]

The timing of attacks is also dependent on the number of blade actions the attack requires. A direct attack that just takes advantage of a perceived weakness in the opponent's defence uses only one blade action, and therefore occurs in one time. A *due tempi* attack will include two blade actions, such as an attack to the head, to draw a defensive response, followed by an attack to the belly in a second time. *Mezzo tempo* refers only to defensive actions (i.e. actions that require a prior offensive action by the opponent).

The timing of *giocco stretto* defences is difficult to define using fencing terminology, because such actions were much rarer when most of the terms were coined. However, every grip, lock or throw should be done while the attacker is still moving forwards, so in the time of his attack. I therefore define all *giocco stretto* defences as *mezzo tempo*. Once the first *giocco stretto* contact is made (such as the grip to the wrist, or the elbow envelopment lock), the continuation of the defence (such as a pommel strike, or a belly cut) is done in a second time. But the grip, lock or throw is an attack, so the initial action is defence and attack in one time; hence a counterattack.

INTENTION, FEINTS, TRUE AND FALSE PLAY

In martial arts circles (Eastern and Western), intention usually refers to the correct alignment of the mind and body towards the accomplishment of your technique. Specifically in Western swordsmanship, it is also used to qualify the nature of a fencing action. First intention, second intention, even third or fourth, may be used by a fencer to create the opportunity for a successful strike. For example, I may attack my opponent expecting to hit him. That is first intention. Or, I may attack my opponent expecting him to counterattack. Having drawn his counterattack, I deflect it and hit him: second intention. Or, perhaps I wish to attack my opponent by hitting him on the head. So I cut. If he defends himself, and I react to his defence, then I am just acting on reflexes, and there is no change of intention. However, if I attack with the intention of drawing his defence (in other words forcing him to do something such as deflect my blade), and I use the opening created by his blade moving in the way of mine, deceiving his deflection, and cutting up at his waist, then I have successfully enacted a second-intention attack.

Against a fencer that prefers *due tempi* defences, it is correct to use a feint to draw that defence and counter it. As Vadi puts it in chapters 12 and 13:

> Feints mean confusion
> which bewilders the other's defense,
> so (that) he can't understand
> what you want to do on (either) side ....
> you can well hammer more and more times
> hitting from one side only
> your feints should go on the other side,
> and as he parries, losing his way,
> you should hammer on the other side;
> then you should evaluate
> which technique to win with.[7]

In historical fencing, the use of feints is often referred to as *false play*: this is because the feint was originally called (in sixteenth-century English-language treatises) a *false* attack. True play, as the name implies, refers to fencing without the use of feints.

To be able to fight, you only need to be able to execute the proper physical actions at speed: to be able to fence, you must also have an intellectual framework for analysing the actions, for describing them, and for explaining how they work. Working through the practical exercises that illustrate each principle, the exercise will clarify the principle, and the principle will clarify the exercise.

THE CROSS

The principle of the cross is fundamental to the longsword, and is expressed in four main ways:

Crossing the sword: the *incrosada*, crossing your opponent's sword with your own, is usually the first defensive action taken. It is referred to repeatedly by both Fiore and Vadi, and is mention by many other later masters too. The correct crossing of the blades is as close to 90 degrees as possible, as this is the safest, "truest" cross.

Crossing his feet: draw an imaginary line between your opponent's feet: any force applied parallel to that line will be easier for him to resist than force applied across it. So when entering into *giocco stretto*, try to cross the line between his feet; apply your force at 90 degrees to that line for maximum effect on his balance. Whenever you step, you should attempt to bisect the line of his movement, and finish on a line that would cross the line between his feet. Refer to the *giocco stretto* exercises to see this principle at work.

Crossing his line: when attacking into his attack, your blade should be crossing the line of his cut: if his cut is descending from your left to your right, your counter should either descend from your right to your left, or ascend from your left to your right, crossing the arc of his cut. See for example the Through-Cutting deflections exercise.

Using the cross: your longsword has a crossguard; the sword is your cross. Keep the crossguard between your opponent's blade and your target, and he cannot hit you. This is best seen in the defensive uses of the guard *frontale*.

Chapter 5
Equipment

To begin the practice of swordsmanship, all you need is a stick. It is perfectly possible to master most longsword technique, and even to successfully fight fully armoured opponents, with a four-foot bit of oak. However, to properly appreciate the character of the weapon, and to employ the full range of techniques in practice and in combat, there is a minimum amount of kit required. Firstly, you need a good steel sword, blunted and bated[1] to be used in pair practice. If you intend to practise at full speed, or to fight, you must also obtain and wear protective gear to prevent accidental injury, and to allow your opponent to use a full range of attacks. You cannot fully assimilate the concepts of control, timing and distance if you cannot actually hit your opponent at speed.

Choosing a Sword
It is important that you decide exactly what you want this weapon for. Is it for fighting, solo practice, pair practice, adornment, or all four? Will it be used for armoured or unarmoured fighting, for duelling or battle re-enactment? In any case, it must be sturdy enough for its most strenuous likely use. Light, fast weapons intended for unarmoured duelling can get damaged on the re-enactment battlefield, and too many people come away from a practice session heartbroken when their shiny wall-hanger[2] has been smashed to bits. There is also the consideration of exact historical accuracy. Always check with your supplier or the manufacturer that the weapon is intended for the use you want it for.[3]

The other major consideration is size. One of the few things that every fencing master appears to agree on is that your weapon should be in proportion to your own size and strength.

In my opinion, the ideal longsword conforms to the following general rules:

- Its total length should be such that with the tip on the floor, the pommel reaches near your sternum. Much shorter, and it should be a single-hander, much longer and it should be a two-hander, or a greatsword.
- The handle should be two and a half to three of your hand-breadths long.
- The crossguard should be about as long as the handle (except when the handle is remarkably long). Usually this means between one and two hand's lengths.
- The balance point should be approximately 3 to 5 fingers (about 2-3½ inches) beyond the crossguard.
- The weight should be such that you can comfortably swing the weapon with one hand if the forefinger is hooked over the crossguard. (Usually 2½-4 lbs: remember that sharp weapons are usually lighter than the equivalent blunt weapon.)

The importance of the balance cannot be overemphasised: a heavy, well balanced sword will be easier to use than a light, poorly balanced one. The major factors governing longevity of the weapon are the quality of the steel used, the design and construction, and the level of craftsmanship. All else being equal, heavier weapons tend to last longer in combat.

In terms of style, it is mainly a case of preference, though in pommel design, for instance, I prefer a tapered pommel to a round one because it extends the effective length of the handle without adding weight to the weapon. The most important thing is to buy the sword that is fit for its purpose and that you really like the look of. If you love it and want to play with it all the time, you will spend more time practising.

If you will be practising and fencing without plate gauntlets (see below), I would advise at least a pair of side rings to protect your hands. In general, I train with a sword with a plain crossguard, to perfect my technique, but freeplay with a similar weapon that has the rings. On the subject of the hilt, if you absolutely must go for a fancy hilt with dragons and the like, and still expect to fence with the weapon, make sure that the manufacturer has used a metal intended for such use. The other problem with fancy hilts (other than their fragility) is that they tend to add unnecessary weight to the weapon. The best compromise, if you can afford it, is to have what we call "fighting kit" and "drinking kit," the former plain and sturdy, the latter as ornamental as you like.[4] This is historically accurate: wealthy gentlemen about town would pose with outrageously figured and jewelled hilts, but go to war with plain steel.

If possible, it is usually best either to have your weapons made to order by a smith you can trust, or to buy in a shop or market where you can examine the workmanship and feel the heft before handing over the cash. If you wish to buy mail-order, I would recommend only buying products that your friends or acquaintances have bought and recommend or will let you try out. And remember, buying one good sword is usually cheaper in the long run than repeatedly buying cheap ones that break. Cost is also relative. If you are going

Figure 5.1: *The author with his two favorite longsword trainers.*

to train for an hour a week, and a sword lasts ten years, then a 520€[5] sword costs 1€ per hour. The same sword, if used for an hour every day, is only 1/7th as expensive (per hour). In general, a good sword from a reasonable Eastern-European smith will cost about 350€, and be perfectly fit for use. A hand-made custom weapon from a European or American smith will cost from around 800€, and the sky is the limit. Bear in mind that not all smiths are historians: do not necessarily take their word for the historicity of any weapon. If you know exactly what you want, send very precise specifications. The best swords I have ever handled come from JT Pälikkö, of Helsinki.[6] He is extremely knowledgeable about the historical record, and an extraordinary craftsman. His weapons cost a lot of money, but you get more than what you pay for. For a tighter budget, I use and sell swords made by Pavel Moc,[7] which have an excellent price-to-quality ratio.[8]

If you intend to wear your sword, it is normally best to use a belt-slung baldrick (see Clayton, for example). Please do not go for the Hollywood-style back-carry, with the sword slung over your back and the handle over your shoulder. It leaves you hopelessly open on the draw (you have to open your centre to draw the weapon, inviting a thrust under the sword-arm). The back-carry cannot be drawn in low rooms, nor does it allow you to use a full length scabbard.[9] A scabbard is advisable to protect the blade from the elements and people's legs and pieces of furniture from the blade. This is not so much of a consideration with blunt weapons. Beware of letting the inside of the scabbard get wet - the moisture will be sealed in and rust your blade to bits.

PARTS OF THE SWORD

Tip to pommel, all parts of the sword have their specific uses. Starting from the pommel:

1. The **pommel** provides a counter-balance to the weight of the blade, dramatically affecting the balance of the sword. It is also very useful as a blunt instrument for pummelling your opponent, usually in the face.
2. The **handle**: this is where you normally grip the sword.
3. The **crossguard** (sometimes known as the quillons, cross, or hilt). This affords vital protection for your hands against your opponent's blade sliding down, and is crucial for many of the defences and closing actions. Vadi specifies that it must be made of strong iron. It can also be used for hitting your opponent, and for applying locks and throws. Parts 1, 2, and 3 are collectively known as the **hilt**.
4. The **false edge**, also called the back edge is towards you, pointing up your right forearm, when holding the sword.
5. The **true edge**, also called the front edge is away from you when you hold the sword.
6. The half of the blade closest to the handle is known as the *forte* (strong), because it is closer to the grip, affording superior leverage when opposed to the *debole* of your opponent's blade. Most deflections and all oppositions should be done with this section.
7. Parts eight and nine combined are known as the *debole* (weak) because they are less effective in defence. Attacks and engagements (deliberate investigative contact with your opponent's blade) are made with the *debole*.
8. The area from the midpoint to the last section is used for cuts. If you whack the flat of the blade with your free hand while holding the sword upright, the blade should vibrate. The point at which the blade is not apparently vibrating is the point of percussion, and that is where the most power is available for cutting. However it tends to be too close to the handle to make full use of the weapon's length, so most cuts are done with the part of the blade just beyond the point of percussion.
9. The last four inches or so are used for thrusts or slashing cuts.

SWORD CARE

Looking after your weapon is largely a matter of keeping it dry, clean, and free of stress risers (a stress riser is a weak point, usually a deep nick, which encourages the blade to fold at that point).

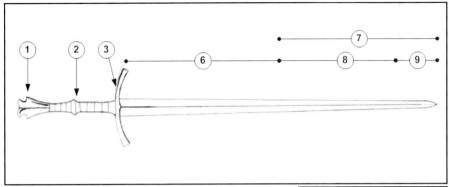

Figure 5.2: *Parts of the longsword*

Figure 5.3:
Parts of the longsword

Occasional rubdowns with a moisture repellent oil and steel wool or bear's tongue,[10] followed by a coat of microcrystalline wax,[11] should keep the blade and hilt clean (follow manufacturer's recommendations if you have a gilt, blued or otherwise ornamented weapon). Do not be afraid to file down any large nicks, and file off any burrs: this is important from a safety perspective, as the blade is most likely to break at a nick, and burrs can be very sharp. Care of sharp weapons is a much bigger subject, and will be covered in a later volume. The edges of a blunt weapon should always be kept smooth enough that you can run your bare hand hard up the edge and not get scratches or splinters. Even the toughest and most cherished sword will not survive repeated abuse: the best guarantor of longevity for your sword (and yourself) is correct technique.

Figure 5.4:
*Stress-riser on a
sword blade
(photo Brian R. Price)*

PROTECTIVE EQUIPMENT

There were some masters who believed that the safest course is to fence with sharp weapons and no protection.[12] This is how it was often done in the past until the invention of fencing masks (though there are tournament records and declarations as early as the 14th century that record the use of blunt practice weapons; King Rene d'Anjou's tournament treatise of 1470 is perhaps the best source of information on such weapons). Such masters are right in theory, in that freeplay with sharps is the best way for students to learn absolute respect for the weapon, and the importance of absolute control. There are a few contemporary masters with whom I will fence like this, and there is nothing like it for generating a perfect fencing approach. But try explaining that to the insurance companies, or in the event of a slip, the police or coroner. It was often said in the eighteenth century that you could tell a fencing master from his eye-

Figure 5.5: *Topi Mikkola in SESH full freeplay kit.*

patch and missing teeth. Never forget that even a blunt blade can break bones. Therefore, when free fencing, or when practicing drills at speed, it is essential that you wear appropriate safety gear. You do this not for your own sake, though self-preservation does come into it, but for the benefit of your training partner. Your protection allows him to hit you safely.

Choosing protection is a very controversial subject. Too little, and you can end up badly hurt (even in practice). Too much, and you can't fence properly. Firstly, it is important to establish what style of fencing you will be doing. If you are practising armoured combat, then buy the best fitting, best made armour that you can from an armourer who knows how you intend to use it and has seen what you want to do. This is the hardest style of fencing to appropriately regulate, because accurate technique requires you to go for the least armoured spots (throat, eyes, armpits, joints), but safety requirements obviously prohibit that.

Figure 5.6: *Equipment recommended for longsword play at SESH.*

The type of longsword fencing that you will learn from this book is unarmoured duelling. For simulating such combat, I recommend and use the following:

1. An FIE[13] standard fencing mask. This allows you to thrust at the face (a very common target), and generally attack the head. This does have three major caveats. Firstly, it leaves the back of the head open, and you must be very careful not to strike at this target. An added apron of thick leather affords some protection. Secondly, it does not protect the head and neck from the wrenching force of over-vigorous blows. It is vital that you and your opponent learn control before engaging in freeplay. Thirdly it is designed to protect the face from high-speed, light, flexible weapons, not slower, heavier, rigid ones. So continually check them for wear, and make absolutely sure that your weapons are properly bated.

2. A steel or leather gorget, or stiff collar, to protect the throat. Points can slip under the bib of a mask and crush the larynx.

3. (For women) a rigid plastic chest guard.

4. A point-resistant fencing jacket rated at at least 500 Newtons.

5. Sturdy, preferably padded and/or armoured gauntlets,[14] which should extend at least four inches past the jacket cuff to prevent points sliding up your sleeve. I have twice had

fingers broken through unpadded mail gloves,[15] and now use a pair of tailor-made fingered gauntlets from K+K art, which cost about 150€. I always wear a pair of padded fencing gloves even when practicing alone.[16] Ice-ball gloves, with leather extensions on the cuffs are a cheap alternative.

6. A padded gambeson, or a plastron.[17] If you are making one yourself, bear in mind that it should be thick enough to take the worst out of the impact of the blows, and prevent penetration from a thrust. All openings should be covered. If the garment opens at the front, the sides should overlap by at least three inches. The collar should be high enough that thrusts coming under the bib of the mask do not make contact with your throat. A plastron must wrap around the ribs, and properly cover the collar bones and shoulders. I usually wear a fencing jacket and plastron (as pictured).

7. A box for men (called a "cup" in the US).You only forget this once.

8. Rigid plastic protectors for the knees and

9. for the elbows, of the sort worn by in-line skaters (worn under the clothes for that period look if you prefer), will save a lot of pain, and some injury.

On the matter of footwear, few practitioners agree. In the longsword treatises, there are no heavy boots, and certainly no built-up heels. For a completely historical style, it is necessary to wear completely accurate period clothing at least occasionally because it can affect the way you move. Training barefoot or in smooth leather soled shoes is the most accurate, and often very slippery, though there is some evidence to suggest that knights, at least, wore shoes with whipcord attached to the soles for better grip.[18] I have fenced on wooden floors, concrete, stone, tarmac, grass and gravel, in sports halls, salles, castles, forests and on hillsides, in all weathers from heatwave to snowstorm, wearing everything from thigh-boots to hiking boots to trainers to period shoes to barefoot, and my conclusion is that it does not matter what you wear on your feet provided that you understand grounding, body-mechanics and footwork. Excessively grippy soles can lead to joint injury as you may stop too suddenly, or get stuck when you should be turning (particularly in falls at *giocco stretto*). The dangers in wearing too slippery soles are obvious. In the salle I usually wear wrestling boots or trainers.

OTHER EQUIPMENT

Without doubt the single most important bit of safety equipment is good common sense. Fence according to the limits of your equipment, exercise control and respect the weapon at all times, and you will never have a serious injury. Minor bumps and bruises come with the territory.

In general with the longsword I do not use training aids such as wooden wasters (dummy swords). For striking targets, I have a student hold an old car tyre. The sound when you hit it varies from a pathetic 'tap' to a wall-shaking 'boom' that lets you know you've got it right (as does the grunt and expression of pain on your assistant's face).

The pell is one of the simplest and most effective training tools ever devised. It is certainly as old as the Romans: Vegetius mentions infantry soldiers "cutting at the post."[19] Simply a post in the ground (with a cross-bar if you want), the idea is to hit the pell as hard and fast as you can without actually touching it (or just tapping it on a marked spot, for accuracy). Under no circumstances should you deliberately hit a solid object with a sword: the shock can damage your joints, and break the sword.[20] Used properly, the pell can teach you power, control, distance and accuracy. Not bad for a cheap bit of timber.

A punchbag can make an excellent cutting and thrusting target. However, punchbags are not normally designed to withstand cuts even from a blunt sword, so it is a good idea to reinforce it with leather or canvas, which can be marked with lines to cut at and dots to thrust at.

For sharp cutting practice, soaked reed mats, tightly rolled, are commonly used, particularly in Japanese swordsmanship, but are quite costly. You can also practice by cutting a piece of dangling rope (one-inch hemp is best), a large plastic bottle filled with water, or drinks cans also filled with water. Sharp cutting practice will be covered in detail in a subsequent book.

Figure 5.7: *Practice with a tyre (front and rear right) and a pell (left rear).*

UNARMED PRACTICE

T he exercises contained in this book are designed to be as accessible as possible to a beginner with little or no experience, and with no access to an instructor. They are structured to show you a range of basic concepts and techniques that can be assimilated reasonably quickly to allow you to fence properly. This is not the way I teach in my Salle. There, all students have regular access to an instructor, and know that they will not be fencing until they are ready. My school method is therefore designed to build up their technical repertoire slowly, and to work more on the manipulation of blade contact, body contact, distance and timing. Put another way, we focus on the transitions between techniques more than on the techniques themselves. That method is useless to a beginner without proper supervision. There are techniques and exercises in this book that many of my students have never seen, because they don't need them; and on the other hand, there are drills that we do in the Salle that would be impossible to adequately describe in a book aimed at beginners.

You will notice that almost all pair work with longswords shown in the photographs are done wearing no mask, jacket or pads. This is how I prefer to teach: under my supervision, my students do all pair work very slowly and carefully, working with total control. When they have got the hang of the basics, and their forms and solo work is looking good at speed, then they kit up and do the drills faster. However, *in the absence of an instructor, I allow no pair practice at all without full protection.* Obviously, I cannot be present when you are practising, but if you are practising my method please observe my rules and *always wear a mask, jacket, gauntlets and pads when training with a partner.* Everybody makes mistakes; anyone can slip, misjudge distance, or have a lapse in concentration. With these weapons, the first mistake can result in serious injury, so guard against it with proper protection.

The practice of the exercises in this book will clarify the general fencing principles; and the principles clarify the techniques. It is a positive feedback loop, so do not worry if at first you don't understand the principles and can't get the techniques right. There is only one way to transfer the idea of a technique from your head (where, no doubt, you are the most accomplished and graceful swordsman alive) to your hands and feet (which generally lag well behind in the grace stakes). That is repetition. Let me say that again. The only way to get good at swordsmanship is to do it a lot. Not just the fun, flashy stuff, but the simple, basic movements which can be tedious to do and unimpressive to look at to the uninformed. The device that allows you to practise these movements until they are right is drill. In other words, the following section comprises a series of drills that will, if practised over and over again, reprogram your body to move like a swordsman. We will begin with the feet, and work up.

WARM-UP
Before beginning the swordsmanship exercises, it is a good idea to warm up. Once you have internalised the correct mechanics and your technique is very good, you will not need to warm up to defend yourself: you can't say: "Hold on Mr. Mugger while I do some stretches so I don't pull a muscle beating the crap out of you." But before that, you will be stressed by even the basic actions. As you get fitter and better trained, the techniques you can attempt will become more demanding, so the warm up remains necessary. Every exercise in the warm-up is as much a body mechanics and breathing exercise as anything else. There are three parts to a good warm-up:

1. Gently loosening the joints, especially the spine
2. Raising core-body temperature, sending blood into the muscles
3. Stretching

Much of the effectiveness of a warm-up is that it reminds the muscles to contract smoothly, using as many muscle fibres as necessary. One of the most common reasons for a training injury is through accidentally forcing insufficient muscle fibres to do the work that would normally be done with more. The exact exercises and stretches should mainly involve the muscle groups you are going to use: there is no point stretching the wrists before a footwork class: do it just before you actually start using your arms.

At SESH we always begin with a warm-up followed by a footwork/body mechanics/unarmed combat session, then move on to weapons practice. (More advanced classes will sometimes go directly to weapons practice after the warm-up, so the warm-up is different.)

At the end of every training session, you should warm-down with ten minutes or so of stretching. When warming down, it is a good idea to hold each stretch for at least 30 seconds, breathing calmly and deeply. Focus on the muscle groups that are normally stiffest in the days after a really vigorous training session.

For a sample warm-up program, see Appendix B.

BODY MECHANICS

The first and most important aspect of learning to use any weapon is precise body control. If you cannot control what your arms and legs do, how can you possibly control the movement of a four-foot length of steel? As usual, the treatises offer detailed guidance if you know where to look. To recap, the drawings in Fiore and Vadi both indicate the imaginative processes that will lead to correct body mechanics. Recall that Fiore used the image of an elephant with a tower on its back. If you imagine your hips and legs to be the elephant, solid, stable and secure, and your back and shoulders to be the tower, you will find that as your back remains straight, it must remain upright whatever your legs are doing, or you will tip over. This will make more sense in the light of some of the exercises to come.

Vadi presents us with a more detailed set of instructions. The feet are on a wheel, where one foot remains still (the tower) and the other goes around it. I do not place too much emphasis on which foot stays still and which goes round because Vadi later shows guards with either foot in the advanced position; when the right foot is forwards, the left must be the sun and the right the tower, if you are to step forwards. As always, the knees are, as Vadi suggests, the keys to correct movement. Specifically, your legs must "open and close;" in other words, bend and straighten.

The use of the longsword is not an ambidextrous art. As the sections on techniques will show, the body is clearly differentiated between right and left. A right-hander will always have his right hand on the grip near the cross-guard, and left free to hold the handle, the blade, or to grapple.[1] This is made abundantly clear not only by the illustrations of technique but also by the apportioning of animal images to the right and left arms and shoulders. The right arm is the dragon. It is deadly and cunning, and kills with impunity. The left hand is the greyhound, legendarily swift in attack. The right shoulder is the bear, which roams the woods, by indirection finding direction out. The left is the ram, which will butt and shove enemies to the ground. And the eye over the heart watches the fight, indicating that your torso should face the direction of your intention. Try to keep these images in mind when practising technique, as they will help you to move correctly and to think out your strategies in the right manner for this weapon.

EXERCISES IN BODY MECHANICS

Body mechanics for martial arts is the study of how to position and move your bones for maximum efficiency. Effectiveness is determined by the ability of any position to withstand pressure, and the ability of any movement to deliver power. These exercises will improve your balance, make you much harder to push over, and strengthen your legs. If you are wondering why you should bother to use an exercise that you will never repeat in free fencing, then consider how many boxers lift weights, and how few take dumbbells into the ring.

GROUNDING

The first requirement of good footwork is a feel for the ground beneath you, and the exact position of your weight. If you have never consciously made yourself aware of these things but taken them for granted, you may still be extremely well coordinated, because usually the body looks after itself with subconscious processes. By making yourself aware of these monitoring processes, you can gain control of them, and thereby find your weaknesses and improve on them. This first exercise is for many students the most important one of all, because it can cure all sorts of later problems with guards, cuts, and movement. Practise this barefoot to start with, and then in whatever footwear you normally practise in.

1. Stand relaxed, with the outside edges of your feet parallel and shoulder-width apart.
2. Bend your knees slightly and let your weight come onto the middle of both feet evenly, keeping your feet firmly flat on the floor.
3. Shift your shoulders back and keep your head up, so your back is straight. Use a mirror or a friend to tell you when your spine is in its natural resting position.
4. Let your arms hang naturally.
5. Close your eyes and feel the weight in your feet. Be aware of how it is supported in the legs. Imagine yourself as heavy as possible, that feeling of weight spreading down into the floor. Visualise your feet growing roots into the ground. Be completely relaxed, but immovable. Keep this up for a few minutes if you can.
6. Without leaning at all, moving only the hips, transfer your weight to the right foot. Do not allow your right hip to rise onto the leg: keep your pelvis completely level. Your right knee will have to bend slightly more to allow this to happen. *Keep your centre of gravity low and your back straight.*
7. When you feel completely grounded through the right foot, and your left foot is still stuck firmly to the floor by the imagined roots, shift back to the middle, slowly and without losing the connection.
8. Repeat the exercise to the left. Finish in the middle.

Five minutes a day spent practising this will solve most balance problems. It can be done at the bus stop, at work, in queues at the supermarket, anywhere at all. With practice, you won't need to close your eyes to get that feeling of groundedness. It is vital that you retain this awareness of the ground, your weight, and how they are connected, whenever you practise.

Figure 6.1:
Proper balance allows for great freedom of movement.

BALANCE

Once you have become comfortable with the first exercise, repeat it to the point where your weight is largely on the right foot. Now, with no upper-body movement, lift the left leg until the thigh is horizontal. Do this with your eyes open at first, then try it with them closed. Most people rely on visual cues for balance: you will probably start to wobble when you can't see. Your body is equipped with alignment sensors (the semi-circular canals in the inner ear); with practice, you can rely on them instead. If you start to lose your balance, lower your weight, and send it down into the ground. Try to keep your head level and still. It may help to look at a point on the wall, then close your eyes but still stare at that point. Practise this exercise on each leg until you can reliably stand on either leg with your eyes shut for a full minute. *The keys to success are persistence, posture, and visualisation.*

THE GUARD POSITIONS/ STANCES

There are basically two stances used with the longsword: forward and rear. The forward stance has the front foot pointing forward, and the weight about 70% on the front foot. This is the most common position, and is used for the guards of *posta longa*, *posta breve*, *posta di dente chinghiale*, and *porta di ferro* (described below).

Figure 6.2: *The forward stance.*

TO FIND THE FORWARD STANCE

1. Stand with the feet together, right foot pointing forwards, left foot pointing to the left and a bit forwards, and an inch gap between the heels
2. Become aware of the ground.
3. Step straight forward with the right foot twenty to thirty inches (51-76cm). Keep your weight low, your back straight, head up and knees bent.

Figure 6.3:
A- *The forward stance.*
B- *The rear stance.*

This is the basic "on guard" position. In it, you are stable, balanced, and ready to move in any direction at any time.

To find the rear stance

1. Stand in the forward stance, right foot forwards.
2. Turn your hips 45 degrees anticlockwise and push your weight 70% onto the back foot, and at the same time pivot the feet on the balls so that the heels shift forwards, the front heel more than the back, leaving the feet parallel, toes pointing backwards at a 45 degree angle. An alternative way to find the rear position is to assume the forward position, right foot forwards, then turn your body (don't move your feet except to turn them) anticlockwise 135 degrees, into a left-foot forwards forward position.

 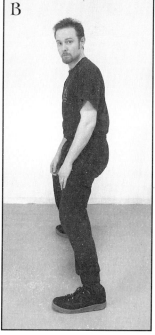

Figure 6.4:
A- *The forward stance.*
B- *The rear stance.*

Figure 6.5:
Testing the stance. Notice in particular how the pelvis remains centered as the pressure increases.

Now look back into the original forwards direction without turning your hips.

In both stances, the back is straight, head up, shoulders relaxed, etc. The turn from forward to rear position is called the *volta stabile* by Fiore.[2]

TESTING THE STANCES

One of the definitions of a good stance is that it can withstand pressure. The most common problem with weak stances is incorrect positioning of the hips and pelvis. To check for the correct position:

1. Stand as in the first grounding exercise.
2. Raise your hands to shoulder height.
3. Curve the base of your spine out so your coccyx (tailbone) is pointing back (stick your bum out).
4. Have your partner push gently against your hands. Your feet should immediately tip up, and you lose your balance.
5. Adjust the position of your coccyx by tucking it under and forwards, and retest your balance.
6. Keep making small alignment adjustments until you find the position in which you can withstand the most pressure (you will not be able to withstand very much because you are being pushed in a direction that is not supported by a foot).

You should find that you can absorb the most pressure when your coccyx is pointing straight down. This is the correct pelvis position for all stances. Now check that your stances are strong with the following exercise:

1. Assume the forward stance
2. Reacquaint yourself with your weight. Ease it back onto your left foot, then forward onto your right, maintaining ground awareness and perfect posture.
3. In this position, have a friend *gently* press your right shoulder: you should be able to route the pressure into your back foot. Your

friend should feel like he is leaning on a rock.

4. Test your balance by having him let go without warning: you should not move at all. In other words, don't push back, just allow the gentle force being applied to make you really conscious of your connection to the ground.
5. Repeat this exercise with the left foot forwards.
6. Repeat this exercise in rear stance

When you can direct the pressure from your shoulder, extend your hand (the right if the right foot is forwards), keeping the elbow low and the arm relaxed, and direct the pressure from there. It is important that you do not tense in the shoulders, but allow your partner's force to flow through you into your back foot. Do not lean into the pressure. The classic mistake here is to allow the shoulder blade to get pushed back. Be careful to keep the elbow down, and the arm extending forwards, allowing the shoulder blade to remain flat. Someone running their hand from one shoulder across your back to the other

should not feel anything sticking out. I often tell my students to imagine reaching for a pint of ale (or beverage of your choice) when extending the arm.

Of course, there is a big difference between grounding in a nicely set-up exercise and doing it in a fight. The important thing to master at this stage is the *awareness* of the ground and your posture. This awareness will allow you to feel whether you are doing the later techniques correctly or not.

Figure 6.6:
Pressure testing exercise.
A- Forward stance.
B- Rear stance.

Footwork[3]

This subject is vast enough to require a book of its own. There are so many possible correct steps, passes, lunges, turns, and combinations that to list them all would serve only to confuse and discourage the beginner. That said, **the essence of good footwork is simply this: push your weight from a bent leg to a bending leg,** or as Vadi put it, the legs must open and close. The basic ideas that govern good footwork are few and simple:

- **posture** which leads to
- **balance** which allows you to generate and deliver
- **power** which must be clearly focused in one of
- **the eight directions**.

With an understanding of these principles, and the ability to step, pass and turn with good grounding and posture, all of the complicated stuff will become easy to work out. You should start with the chapter on body mechanics, and practise the exercises there before attempting the footwork techniques. There is no way to master footwork without previously mastering grounding and posture control. Many swordsmen have mastered grounding without doing specific exercises, but it probably took them a lot longer than necessary.

Posture

Good posture is vital (remember the elephant!). Refer to the previous exercises, and keep in mind the following guidelines.

- Keep your back upright. However low your stance, do not lean forwards. It puts your head nearer to your opponent's attack, strains your back, makes you less able to change direction, and in general may be considered a Very Bad Thing.
- The leading thigh, shin and foot MUST be in line with the direction that your weight is travelling in. This is for two reasons:
    1. The knee is very strong in one direction: it can bend like a hinge with no problems, but is very vulnerable to being twisted. With the correct alignment, it is perfectly possible to have a very large student stand on the top of your knee while you're in a lunge (don't try this at home!). Correct alignment prevents injury.
    2. A forward-pointing knee and foot maximise your reach.[4]
- Your hips and pelvis must be aligned correctly.
- **Never sacrifice your guard position**: never over-extend, lean into a cut, or lean back away from an attack. As a beginner, it is better to lose every fencing match than to develop bad postural habits.

Balance

Balance is the fundamental principle that underlies the physical, mental and spiritual practice of the art of swordsmanship. In terms of footwork, it is the main diagnostic tool for analysing your technique: if the movement leaves you in perfect balance from start to finish, without muscular strain, it is well done. The slightest wobble is a clear indication that something has gone wrong somewhere. Good physical balance is largely a matter of posture and grounding.

POWER

At a beginner level, power is simply a matter of using as little effort as possible to achieve your aims. The muscular power available to you is the differential between the resting state and full contraction of the muscle. Power can be increased by working both ends of the differential: increasing the strength of the maximum contraction, and reducing the level of contraction in the resting state (a stiff muscle is already using up some of its strength). In other words, the key to power is healthy, toned muscle that has a completely relaxed resting state and can withstand rapid contraction.

We have all heard about people who, under hypnosis or extreme duress, have accessed "superhuman" strength. By and large, that is because most normal muscular contraction is inefficient: not all the fibres contract, and if they do, they are out of synch. This is in part a protective mechanism, since your muscles have the strength to contract so hard and so fast that they can rip your tendons from the bone and destroy your joints. So most people do not need to put on much muscle to increase their power; rather, they need to co-ordinate the muscles they have, and to strengthen the joints to allow the muscles to exert more force safely.

Power in footwork derives from using the large muscles of the legs and buttocks, not the small ones of the back, to push your weight around. In other words, do not fall into a step, *push* into it.

THE EIGHT DIRECTIONS

All steps are executed in one of the eight directions.[5] These are straight forwards, straight back, left, right, diagonally forwards left and right, and diagonally backwards left and right (see page 56).

This image, from Achille Marozzo's *Arte della Armi* (1540), shows two swordsmen engaged on guard, standing on what appears to be a compass. This is because mastery of the sword always requires mastery of the eight directions.

Without command of the directions, it is impossible to reliably control distance, and therefore timing. The zero point, where these directions intersect, depends on the type of footwork you are doing. In general longsword practice they intersect at the middle of the front foot.[6] The importance of the directions and their point of intersection will become clear in later exercises.

These directions need to be named: some martial arts instructors use north, south etc. (I used to, until my Finnish students complained that it was hard enough being taught in English without such non-standard use of normal words. I now use the figure on page 57).

There are of course an infinite number of possible directions. The purpose of restricting yourself to eight is twofold. Firstly, all attacks close distance; whatever direction it comes from, assuming that the swordsmen are facing each other, the attack must shorten the line of direction. Even if he is attacking on the diagonal, he must still close distance. This is over-simplified, but for the purposes of getting a basic idea about how direction relates to distance, imagine that all attacks are coming from long range along the line of direction

Figure 6.7:
The Compass from Achille Marozzo's 1540 treatise, Arte della Armi.

(in free fencing, relatively few of the attacks should come down that line, but it is the easiest to visualise). In response to this hypothetical attack, you have nine useful footwork options.

- You can close in directly, going forwards. This puts you in range for grappling and pommelling.
- You can close in diagonally, going Front Right or Front Left. This puts you in blade range of his body.
- You can sidestep Left or Right. This puts you in blade range of his sword-arm.
- You can step Back, keeping him at a distance.
- You can step diagonally Back Left or Back Right, keeping him at a distance, and forcing him to change direction before he can redouble his attack.
- You can stand your ground.

If you step in a direction that is between any of the eight, say Front-Front Right, for example, you do not close the range enough for grappling or pommelling, and are too close to use the blade effectively. In other words, command of direction is one of the key tools that allows you to effectively command distance. In practically all combat situations, the only useful options will involve one or more of the eight directions.

In addition, careful practice in the eight directions will allow you to understand intuitively the directional components of your opponent's attacks. You will then be able to judge where he is going and what are the useful repsponses. There is also the aspect of general control: if you confine yourself to the eight directions in practice, you will become accustomed to being very precise about where you step, so you will eventually be able to put yourself wherever you want.

Tне Eıgнт Dırections

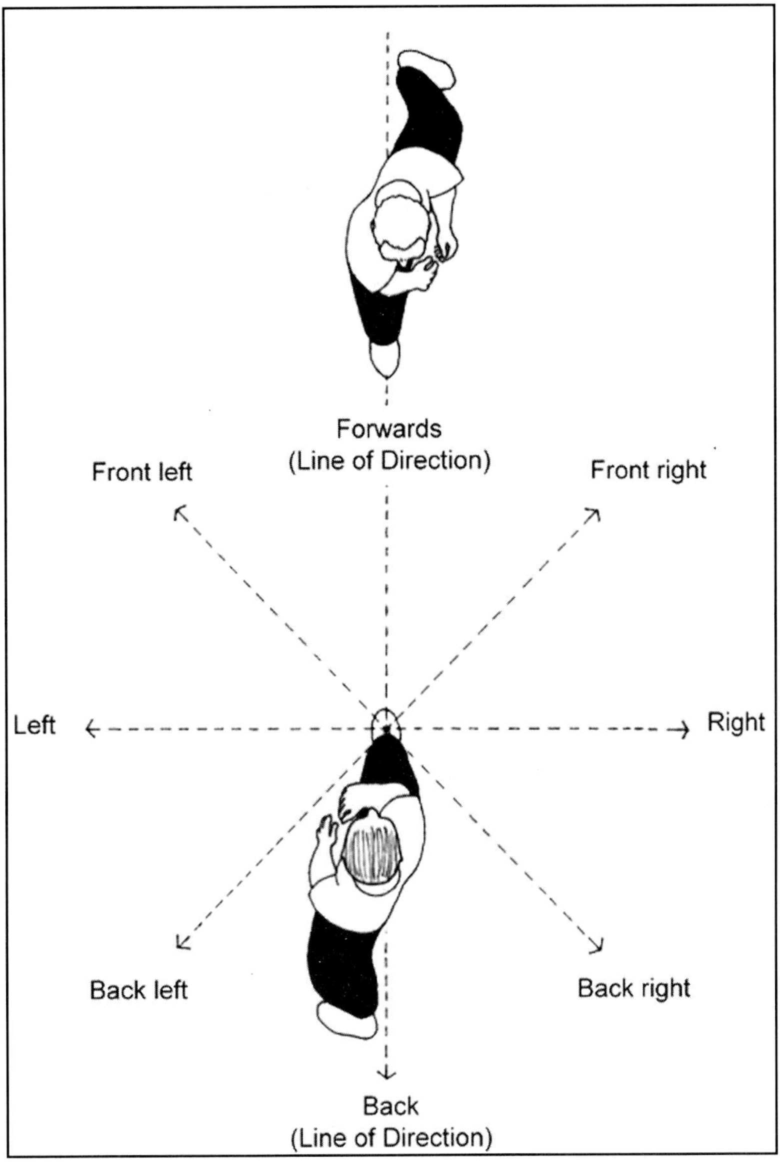

Figure 6.8: *The eight directions of movement, distilled from various Italian treatises.*

Remember that all actions are defined by distance, time, configuration and direction. Before you can reliably manipulate distance and your opponent's direction, you must first be able to control your own.

FOOTWORK EXERCISES

STEPPING

The step is the means by which you make small adjustments in distance, without changing your guard position.

To step forwards (*acressere* in Fiore's system; literally, getting bigger. This is because you get closer to your opponent without changing your configuration):

1. Assume the forward stance.
2. Push your weight forwards and step a few inches with your front foot.
3. Bring up your back foot immediately, exactly the same distance as your front foot moved, so your stance remains the same.

To step backwards (*discressere* in Fiore's system; literally, to get smaller. This is because you go further away from your opponent without changing your configuration):

1. Assume the forward stance.
2. Push your weight backwards and step a few inches back with your back foot.
3. Bring back your front foot immediately, exactly the same distance as your back foot moved, so your stance remains the same.

The most common problem people have with stepping is controlling the direction of their front foot: it has a tendency to turn, usually inwards. Be careful to end how you start: front foot, knee and thigh all going Forwards.

When you have a fair grasp of stepping forwards and backwards, try doing it with direction changes: step Forwards, then turn in the hips and step Front Right, for instance. At all times, keep your head up, back straight, and knees bent.

When you have the hang of the step, and are in control of your weight movement, step in groups of five, three forward, two back, then two back and three forward. Then 2 forward, 1 back, 3 forward, 2 back, 4 forward, 3 back, 5 forward, 4 back until you run out of space or your legs complain too loudly.

There are some historical fencers who believe that longsword footwork is basically the same as normal walking. I agree that this becomes the case after years of practice, when the guard positions, good balance and movement have become completely internalised. However, it is misleading for beginners. I believe it is best to establish correct guards, as they appear in the treatises, and to learn to move between them maintaining a proper defensive position, before becoming too casual about your footwork.

LINEAR PASSING

Passing is the action of one foot going past the other in any direction. Normal walking is one version of it. Having practiced being in the forward stance with either foot forward, you can imagine the process of passing from one side forward to the other. (Fiore's *meza volta*).

1. Starting with forward stance, right foot forward, press most of your weight forwards.
2. As your weight passes over your right foot, pivot it on the ball, swivelling the right heel forwards forty-five degrees clockwise.
3. Step directly forwards into a stable forward stance with the left-foot forwards. Your hips must turn with the motion, and they control your weight, so when you are used to the foot motion, *direct* the pass with your hips.

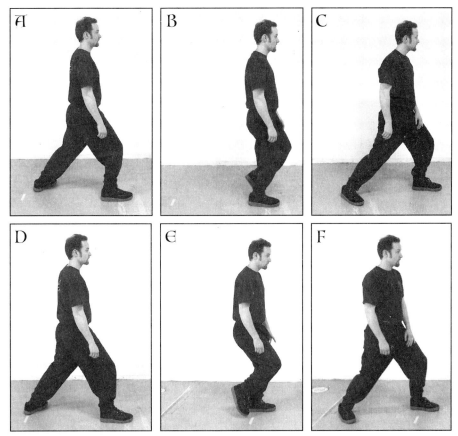

Figure 6.9: *The linear passing step, executed from the forward stance (A). B-The rear foot passes forward, the weight pivoting on the ball of the foot. C-The final rest position, a reverse of fig. 6.9a. D-F represent a retreating passing step, the forward foot moving to the rear.*

This step must be fluid, your weight must not rise and lower. Keep the legs bent, and whichever foot is forwards should be pointed directly forwards, as should your leading thigh. You will find that the direction of this manoeuvre is determined by your passing knee and foot. Angle the foot in a different direction, and your weight will have to follow it. Though your hips do turn, the imaginary central point of your body, about two inches below your navel, travels in a straight line forwards.

Accurate footwork is a combination of foot, knee, and hip control. They must all work together in the same direction if you are to step accurately.

During this step, be absolutely focused on the direction Forwards.
Now practise it again, this time stepping Front Right. Feel how different the movement is: there is a much greater turn in the hips and lead foot.

Practise passing into all eight directions: do not forget to move with the body first, then feet. Eventually it will be as if you are floating: able to move in any direction, grounded and in balance, just by pushing your hips in that direction. Be very, very careful about which direction you are going in, and very, very careful to remain grounded and in perfect balance throughout.

STANCE STEPPING

This is an important exercise as it teaches you to generate power every time you move between rear stance and forward stance.

1. Begin in forward stance.
2. Push your weight back, turning your hips and feet into rear stance.
3. Turn the hips forwards, and return to forward stance.
4. Step through with a pass, so that you end up in forward stance, with the other foot leading.
5. Repeat the exercise from position 4 (i.e. on the other side).

Simple enough, but remember that your back remains relaxed and straight, and that your weight must move smoothly and economically. When you have the basic step-by-step choreography right, the real exercise begins. All three parts are now done in one smooth action, the weight spirals back, turns, and surges forward, driving the step. In effect, it feels like the move to rear stance is winding up a spring, which is suddenly released.

Stance Stepping

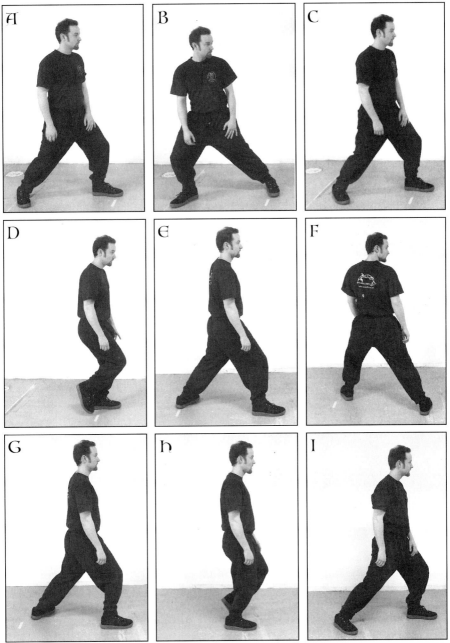

Figure 6.10: *"Stance stepping."*

Figure 6.11:
Simplified rendition of Fillipo Vadi's signo, clearing showing the feet upon the wheel.

CIRCULAR PASSING

There are two kinds of movement between which you need to be able to distinguish: when your centre of gravity moves in a straight line (in whatever direction), and when it moves along a curve. In the above exercises, you have been stepping in a straight line. There will be times, particularly when cutting or throwing, when you will want to move circularly, as suggested by Vadi's wheel. This is achieved by sending your unweighted foot out in a curve forwards.

CIRCULAR PASSING EXERCISE

In this exercise, imagine that the directions are drawn on the ground before you begin, so they do not change. In normal fencing, of course, the directions follow you as you move, so you would always be facing forwards.

1. Assume forward stance, left foot forwards, facing Forwards.

2. Swing your right foot in an arc 180 degrees anticlockwise forwards, pushing your weight onto it as you do so.

3. You are now facing Left, with your weight on the right foot, and both feet pointing Left.

4. Swing your left foot in an arc 180 degrees anticlockwise, placing it behind you.

5. You are now in forwards stance facing Back (and have completed what Fiore calls a *tutta volta*).

6. Turn your hips and feet anticlockwise Forwards, pushing your weight Forwards onto your left foot as you do so. You are now in forward stance, left foot forwards, facing Forwards, as at the start.

7. Repeat the exercise going clockwise, by beginning with the right foot forwards.

Try passing backwards and forwards along a line in this manner: first clockwise forwards, then anticlockwise backwards; then anticlockwise forwards and clockwise back, then changing the direction of the turn in each step. It is important not to lumber along here: keep the weight low and under control. Imagine there is a glass ceiling above your head: do not bounce up and down during these steps. The first time you use a turning step to throw someone effortlessly across a room, you will see why it is worth practising.

Of course, you can use this type of step in every direction. Practise turning into every one of the eight directions, with either foot, from either start position. The key to circular stepping is the feeling that your weight is travelling in a curve.

THE IDEAL STEP (135/90)

Wouldn't it be wonderful if there was a way to fence from a position where you can hit him, but he can't hit you? Well, there is. This step will become very important in the later drills but must be mastered alone first. As with the circular stepping exercise, for clarity the directions are as if drawn on the floor, and do not change during the exercise.

THE IDEAL STEP (135/90) EXERCISE

1. Assume forward stance, left foot forwards.
2. Pass circularly 135 degrees anticlockwise, Front Right .Your right foot should now be pointed Front Left (see fig. 6.13a).
3. Bring your left foot circularly around 90 degrees anticlockwise, forming a normal forwards stance with the right foot forwards, facing Front Left (see fig. 6.13b).
4. Pass linearly forwards with the left foot, into forwards stance, left foot forwards, still facing Front Left.

Figure 6.13:
135/90 exercise and directions of movement.

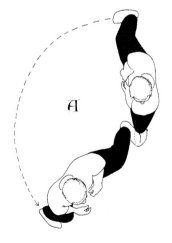

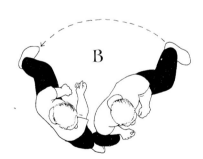

If this sequence is repeated four times, (the next step will be into the original direction Forwards, etc.) you should finish facing Back: repeated eight times, and you are facing the same direction that you started in. You may check the accuracy of your angles by doing this exercise with your eyes shut. Direction should not necessarily be dependent on visual cues. The magic of this step is that if your opponent has attacked linearly in correct distance, and you time this step to his attack, at step 3, you are exactly in distance to cut his body, whereas he cannot reach yours without turning.

FREE FOOTWORK

The above exercises are there to help you develop precise control of your feet, knees and weight. Only when you are able to move fluidly in all directions without loss of balance, are you ready to trust your natural footwork style. Then you can forget all the steps, and just practise directions, in whatever style suits you.

The basic rule of footwork is this: never sacrifice your guard position. So whenever you move, you must move from a perfect position, through a perfect position, to a perfect position. This is achieved by pushing the weight from a bent leg to a bending leg, while keeping the back straight, and maintaining a solid connection to the ground.

WEIGHT

In every longsword guard, and during every step or turn, your weight should be on the balls of your feet. This allows you to pivot easily. It is even possible to do every action with both heels actually off of the ground. The heel of the rear or un-weighted foot in particular should be allowed to rise.

CHAPTER 7

ARMED PRACTICE
SOLO DRILLS

HOLDING THE SWORD: THE GRIP

having warmed-up and practiced your footwork, it is time to apply some of that power and control to actually moving your weapon around. The interface between you and your sword is your grip upon it, and this must be right or you will lack power and control, and may injure yourself. Most people are right handed, so this book is written with all instructions for right-handers. Left-handers can transpose all instructions to suit them: left hand by the crossguard, right hand on the pommel, etc. Where necessary, additional instructions will be given. Leaving aside some of the more advanced half-sword and special-purpose grips, the correct grip in this style is:[1]

Your dominant hand should grasp the handle as close to the cross-guard as possible, with all fingers closed around the handle. A properly-made handle will be shaped such that it fits in the hand and allows you to feel where your

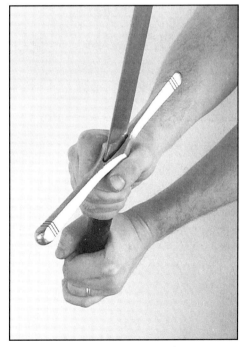

Figure 7.1:
The Standard Grip.

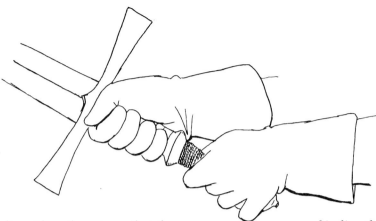

edge lies. Align the grip so that the cross-guard is directly above and parallel to your forearm. This means that the edge is supported by the bones of your arm. Once you have this grip, do not change it at all until you have mastered the basics, and are practicing the more advanced half-sword techniques. The non-dominant hand should grip the handle as far down as possible: if you can, hold the pommel. This maximises the available leverage. It is not wrong to hook a finger over the cross-guard, shifting your grip closer to the point of balance. This makes it easier to control the sword. But it also exposes your finger to possible damage, and should be reserved for when you are so tired you really need the extra help. The sword should be held firmly but not tightly. You are not strangling a chicken. A soft, resilient hold is ideal. This is the only grip used in this book.

GUARD POSITIONS

A guard is first and foremost a position with certain offensive and defensive capabilities that you understand and can therefore use. The importance of various guard positions was emphasised by the masters of old. Every Italian treatise on swordsmanship before Agrippa's of 1553 contained a number of named guards, specifying foot, hand and blade positions. Apparently similar guards (called *poste*), such as Fiore's *posta di dente chinghiale* and *porta di ferro mezana*, were evidently considered entirely different positions. All movements in longsword fencing should be from one guard to another: so when you cut, thrust, recover, deflect, block or manoeuvre, you are always transitioning between correct guard positions. It therefore follows that you need to know these positions, and fully understand what each has to offer, if you are to fence correctly.

The Getty manuscript divides the longsword guards into three different types: *stabile*, *instabile*, and *pulsativa*. These distinctions effectively determine the tactical uses of the guard in question.

Stabile: "stable" guards, as the name implies, are stable positions to fight from.

Pulsativa: "pulsing" guards are those from which the first defensive response is to hit the incoming sword (i.e. give it a pulse).

Instabile: "unstable" guards are transitional positions, which exist (usually) only for the briefest instant as you pass through them.

The most commonly-used guards are these:

Stabile	Pulsativa	Instabile
Posta breve	Tutta porta di ferro	Posta longa
Coda lunga distesa	Posta di donna	Posta di fenestra
Dente di chinghiale		Posta frontale
Porta di ferro mezana		

All of these guards except *denti di chinghiale* and *Tutta porta di ferro* can be taken right foot forward or left foot forward, with the blade on the right side (dextra), or the left side (sinistra).

Essentially, any position you take can be a guard if you understand its tactical and practical consequences. The nine I emphasise here are chosen from Fiore's main twelve because they are the most commonly useful, and the easiest to understand. The questions to ask yourself when in any position are:

- Am I covered? In other words, what part of the body, if any, is protected by the sword in the position it is in. Sometimes the body will be entirely open to attack.
- What attacks can I comfortably launch from this position?
- What lines of attack can I easily cover from this position?
- Can I attack directly from here, or do I have to contract first?
- Where is the threat likely to come from?
- How would I attack someone holding this position?

Some guards are excellent for close distance; some are more useful at longer range. Practice the guards as static positions, then by moving between them, with and without stepping.

POSTA BREVE
Short Position

Posta breve
(short position):
with the blade pulled back.

Figures 7.2:
Guy Windsor in posta breve.
Fiore dei Liberi PD figure 19A, fig. 1.

Coda Longa Distesa
Long Lying Tail Position

Posta di coda lunga distesa
(long-lying tail position):
with the sword all the way behind
you.

Figures 7.3:
Nikodemus Siivola in
coda lunga distesa.
Fiore dei Liberi PD figure 19A, fig. 3.

Dente di Chinghiale
Boar's Tooth

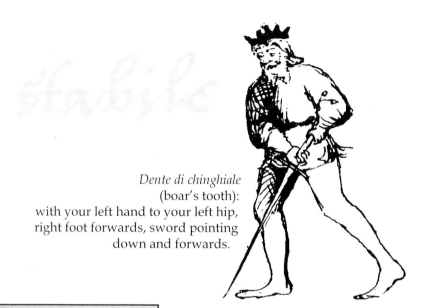

Dente di chinghiale
(boar's tooth):
with your left hand to your left hip,
right foot forwards, sword pointing
down and forwards.

Figures 7.4:
Ilkka Hartikainen in posta denti di chinghiale.
Fiore dei Liberi PD figure 18B, fig. 4.

Porta di ferro Mezana
Iron Door, Middle Position

Porta di ferro mezana
(iron door, middle position):
with the blade pointed down at the
floor.

Figures 7.5:
Auri Poso in posta di porta di
ferro mezana. *Fiore dei Liberi PD
figure 18A, fig. 4.*

TUTTA PORTA DI FERRO
Complete Iron Door

*Porta di ferro mezan*a
(complete iron door):
with the blade pointed down at
the floor.

Figures 7.6:
Antti Kuparinen in posta
di Tutta porta di ferro.

Posta di Donna
Woman's Guard

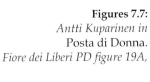

Posta di Donna
(woman's guard):
standing in rear position with the
sword held over your rear shoulder.
There are several variations on this
position in Fiore's treatises: this is
the standard, most versatile one.

Figures 7.7:
Antti Kuparinen in
Posta di Donna.
Fiore dei Liberi PD figure 19A,

Woman's Guard, left side

Figures 7.8:
Antti Kuparinen showing Posta di Donna Sinestra *(the woman's guard, left side).*

Posta Longa
Long Position

Posta Longa
(Long Position):
with the sword pushed forward. This is
the position through which you cut, and
into which you thrust; it represents the
fullest extension of the attack.

Figures 7.9:
*Guy Windsor
in posta longa.
Fiore dei Liberi PD
18B, fig. 1.*

POSTA DI FENESTRA
Window Position

Posta di Fenestra
(window position):
sword pointed forwards, hands at the level of the face, blade horizontal. This guard is primarily used defensively, as a sheltering position to slough off or collect an incoming attack.

Figures 7.10:
Rami Laaksonen in
posta di fenestra.
Fiore dei Liberi PD figure 18A, fig.

Figures 7.11:
Rami Laaksonen in
posta di fenestra *on the left.*

79

POSTA FRONTALE
Coronet or Frontal Position

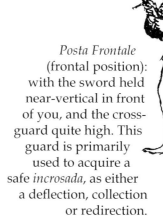

Posta Frontale (frontal position): with the sword held near-vertical in front of you, and the cross-guard quite high. This guard is primarily used to acquire a safe *incrosada*, as either a deflection, collection or redirection.

Figures 7.12: *Guy Windsor in* posta frontale. *Fiore dei Liberi PD figure 18A, fig. 2.*

Figures 7.13:
Guy Windsor
in posta frontale *towards*
the right side.

Some guards are excellent for close distance; some are more useful at longer range. Practice the guards as static positions, then by moving between them, with and without stepping.

ATTACKS

Any action with the sword that directly threatens your opponent or is intended to injure, is an attack. To begin with, most attacks are cuts or thrusts. Modern fencing terminology includes *attack*, which is the first offensive action of a bout, *counter-attack*, which is an attack into your opponent's prior attack, *preparation*, which is an action designed to open the way for an attack (such as knocking your opponent's weapon aside with your own), and *compound attack*, which is an attack including one or more feints. Ultimately fencing matches usually end with one or more cuts, thrusts, or strikes with the hilt. The purpose of this chapter is to train you to make those final actions effectively. Strikes with hands, feet, knees, elbows, head, and armour will be covered in a later book. Attacks may usefully be divided into cuts (blows done with the edge), thrusts (blows done with the point), and hilt-strikes (blows done with the pommel or crossguard).

CUTS

The cut is the most frequently used method of attack with the longsword. In the treatises they are referred to as *colpi* which is more literally interpreted as "blows" or "strikes", which gives the (correct) impression that they are generally executed as solid, powerful, hits, not slashing, raking cuts. I prefer to use the term "cut" to emphasise that the sword has a sharp blade and must be used accordingly. A cut in this system is basically a hard, fast strike with the edge of the weapon, that may then be drawn or pushed to increase the damage.

In my opinion it takes a minimum of ten thousand cuts to begin to understand the subject.[2] And by that I mean ten thousand careful, correctly executed cuts in each of the six main lines, done with a properly balanced steel weapon, either to the air or against the pell. Then ten thousand cuts with a blunt steel weapon against a resilient target that you can really *hit*,[3] in each of the six main directions, then another ten thousand with a sharp weapon against a cutting target. In all, 180,000 repetitions. And that's just a start. Sorry. I never said this was easy or quick. But that is still only 100 cuts per day for five years, or 500 cuts per day for a year, so don't get discouraged.

The physics behind a simple cut is extraordinarily complex, and a complete explanation would be useless to almost all readers. For the purposes of understanding how to cut better, you need only consider these factors:[4]

- The **impact** exerted by the blade on the target, which is affected by
- The **speed** of the edge. Impact is the release of the kinetic energy of the blow. The kinetic energy (E) is proportional to the mass, but proportional to the square of the speed ($E = \frac{1}{2}mv^2$). Therefore it is directly proportional to the mass (m)

of the impacting body: treble the weight of your sword, and you treble the force of the blow. But treble the speed, and the energy on impact is multiplied by nine. Correct handling of the sword allows for very much faster cuts.

- The **mass** of the blade, plus any body-weight you can put behind it. Impact is proportional to the mass (m) of the impacting body, in this case the sword/swordsman combination. It is commonly held that putting your body-weight behind your cut increases it effectiveness by increasing its speed. This is true, but while it is possible to cut only fractionally faster with correct body movement (most of the speed comes from the hands), correct body mechanics allows you to increase the effective mass of the weapon from about 3lb (the sword) to over 10lb (sword, arm and shoulder), hence increasing the impact. My feeling is that it is possible to put about half of your total body weight behind the blow, creating an effective mass of about 80lb. This results in a dramatically harder cut.

- The **force** behind the weapon after impact. A surface impact, however powerful, will do little: the blade must penetrate. This is achieved by providing force (F) behind the weapon, which is done by making sure that the blade is accelerating (a) at the moment of impact, with sufficient body-weight behind it (F=ma).

- The **elasticity** of the sword and of the attacking blade/body combination. The ideal impact of your sword against your opponent is inelastic: he does not yield to the blow, and you do not bounce off. Try cutting a dangling strand of cotton with a very sharp knife. It is very hard to sever the cotton because the cotton yields to the blade. Of course, you can't always hold your opponent still when hitting him, but the inertia of his body is usually sufficient to resist the blow enough to allow the necessary damage. The point of percussion is the part of the blade which vibrates least when the blade is struck: hitting with that spot creates the least elastic impact, hence the most efficient, and most powerful blow. Proper cutting technique does not allow the attacking sword or swordsman to yield to the impact: since the energy has to go somewhere it is directed into the target.

- **Slicing**. There are three ways of cutting: the "down-right blow," a solid chop with the blade; the push cut, where the edge is pushed across the target, and the draw cut, where the edge is pulled across the target. Moving a sharp edge across a target is more effective for penetrating soft tissue than chopping: try it with a sharp blade and a tomato. But slicing does relatively little to a hard target, such as bone. The ideal cut comprises a great impact, to damage the hard tissue, and a slice, to damage the soft tissue.[5] Used properly, a longsword can cut off a limb.

- The **surface area** of the contact. The purpose of an edge is to deliver the available force to the minimum surface area, maximising the pressure (e.g. in pounds per square inch) on the target. Decreasing the surface area of the impact by sharpening the sword and/or curving the cutting edge dramatically increases the penetrative power of the cut. Halve the area of the cutting edge in contact with the target and we can double the effect of the cut. However, good technique is very important: any difference between the plane of the cut and the plane of the blade will cause the blade to twist, dramatically reducing its penetrative ability, and possibly causing a slap with the flat instead of a clean cut. It should also be noted that not all longswords were very sharp, and the blade was not necessarily uniformly sharpened. A completely blunt area beyond the crossguard, and extending for many inches down the blade, was quite common (and called a *ricasso*). Half-sword technique (where the sword is gripped with one hand on the hilt and the other on the blade) does require that the edge being held is not razor sharp. And the sharper the edge, the more damage it will sustain when blocking or deflecting (or being blocked or deflected).[6]

When practicing your cuts, bear in mind that you must strive to create a fast-moving blade, an inelastic impact, and provide force to traverse your edge across and through the target. For pure impact, the tip of the sword is the best part to hit with because it is moving fastest. However, consider the process of cutting through the target. Cutting with the tip is less likely to produce a deep wound. Also, when cutting with the tip the leverage is working against you. To push through you would ideally use the part of the blade closest to the hand (think of whittling sticks with a penknife). This is obviously impractical. The correct cut is a compromise between **impact**, deriving from **speed** and **mass**, and **force** available after impact, derived from your **groundedness**, your forward **momentum**, and the **leverage** working for or against you. There is also the tactical question of how close you want to get to your target before you hit it. For hacking off limbs, use the point of percussion, but for fast cuts to the head, use the last couple of inches of the blade. The best compromise for general purposes with a longsword is to hit with the point about three quarters down the blade, just beyond the point of percussion. This provides plenty of impact, a reasonably controllable shock, and the option to push or pull the blade through.

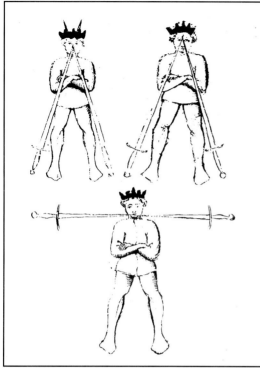

Figures 7.14:
Cutting illustrations from Fiore dei Liberi's Flos Duellatorum, *c. 1409, showing strikes to* fendente, sottani, *and* mezani.

Both Fiore and Vadi describe six cuts and the thrust, as shown left. For the sake of maintaining the Italian flavour of the practice, and to remind students of the historical source of the style, we use Fiore's system for naming the cuts. It is necessary to specify forehand and backhand, so cuts delivered from your strong side (right for right-handers) are *mandritti*,[7] and those delivered backhand are termed *roversi*. This is one convention that is remarkably consistent throughout most treatises, and has survived into modern Italian usage in sports like tennis.[8] For convenience in certain drills, and to provide a common system through all weapons, we also number the cuts 1-6 (in later systems that include vertical cuts, cut 7 is straight down, cut 8 is straight up).

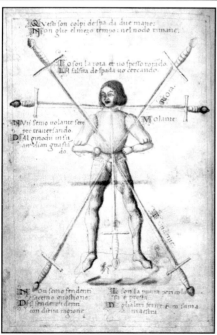

Figure 7.15:
Cutting diagram from Filippo Vadi's Di Arte Gladiatoria Dimicandi. *Photo courtesy the Biblioteca Nazionale, Rome.*

SESH Cutting Diagram

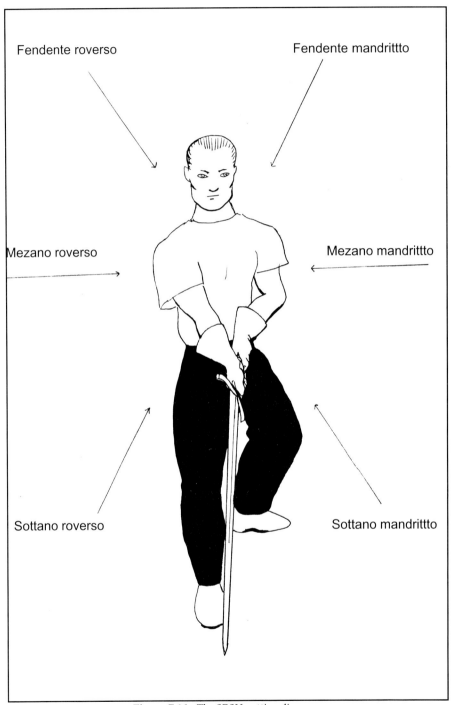

Figure 7.16: *The SESH cutting diagram.*

CUTTING EXERCISES

The process of learning to cut with a longsword is extremely important. The exercises below are designed to work on three levels: mechanics (how to drive the weapon correctly); lines of attack (where to drive it to); and defence (how to do the first two without getting hit). Practice these exercises diligently until the weapon will always go exactly where you want it to, and will do as much damage (or as little) as you choose.

In all cutting exercises, the hands should be pushed forwards, the elbows never locked, and at the point of contact, the wrists must be straight to support the impact that would come from hitting the target.

LEVER ACTION

The purpose of this exercise is to get you used to using the handle as a lever.

1. Assume the guard *posta longa*.
2. Holding the right hand still, push the left hand forwards. This lifts the point.
3. Keeping the right hand still in the same place, pull the left hand back: the point will drop.
4. Stop the blade in the centre of your imaginary opponent's chest.
5. Practice this action repeatedly, directing the angle of the cut into each of the six cutting angles by rotating the right arm like an axle.

Figure 7.17:
Levering the sword.

In this exercise, it should be clear that the power is coming from the left hand, the direction from the right. These cuts can be made with the true edge or with the false edge, in all of the lines (though the false edge *fendente* is rarely used outside the German style). Be very clear about your lines. The edge must not describe a curve, neither should you allow the *fendente* and *sottani* cuts to become too vertical. If the *sottani* cuts are too vertical, you cannot grip the sword properly. Both wrists must remain straight whenever you cut.

When the blade moves backwards, you may find that the crossguard is bashing you on the arm. It is necessary to adjust the angle slightly to allow it to pass on the inside or outside of the wrist, in this and all subsequent exercises. When the cut itself is executed, the crossguard must be again in line with the forearm.

THROUGH CUTS

Through-cuts are made by drawing the weapon entirely through the line of the cut. The purpose of this exercise is to train your hands to direct the true edge into any line, and keep that line consistent from start to finish.

1. Assume the position in 7.18a, with the sword held high over your right shoulder.
2. Cut directly (i.e. with no preparation, just drop the hands) diagonally downwards *fendente mandritto* with the true edge leading, finishing in the position shown in 7.12b.
3. Turn the sword so that the true edge is pointing back up the way you came, and cut up *sottano roverso* as shown in 7.12d.
4. Repeat this exercise ten times, cutting smoothly up and down that one line.
5. Change line, and repeat up and down the *sottano roverso - fendente mandritto* line 7.18h - 7.18f.
6. Change line, and cut laterally across and back the *mezano mandritto - mezano roverso* line shown in 7.18i - 7.18l.
7. Repeat the exercise, but at steps 3,5 and 6 do not turn the hands: cut *sottano roverso*, *sottano mandritto*, and *mezano roverso* with the false edge instead.

Be careful to describe beautiful, clean straight lines, in the angles shown on the cutting diagram. The sword must not wobble, and the lines must not curve at all.

When cutting *sottano* it is very important to keep to the correct diagonal line. Most beginners have a tendency to bring the weapon up too close to the vertical, which forces the left wrist in particular to twist.

Figures 7.18:
Through cutting exercise.

MULINELLI

The *mulinello* (literally "windmill," but in traditional English fencing terminology this action is known as a "compass") requires some explanation. It is not specifically mentioned in Fiore or Vadi's treatises, though there are techniques in *Flos Duellatorum* that look to me like a *mulinello* used as a defensive deflection followed by a cut, and Vadi's *rotare* cuts imply a whirling action.[9] The *mulinello* was not always so called even in Italian treatises. In any case, it is an essential skill. The idea is to whirl the blade around its centre of gravity (the point of balance), creating momentum for your strike. *You must not whirl the sword around your head. It opens you up completely to a counter-attack.* When executing the *mulinelli*, bear in mind that you must always protect the centre. Keep the *forte* always in front of you where it will protect you.

MULINELLO EXERCISE
1. Keeping your hands below shoulder height, push the left hand up and forwards, lowering the weapon point down over your right thigh, with the true edge out. You are now holding the sword upside down.
2. Continue the circular motion of the blade by pulling the left hand towards you, and pushing the right hand forward, sending the point in an arc forwards, with the true edge away from you. In other words, the sword-point describes a full vertical circle on your right hand side.

Remember that every turn of the blade is driven by a smaller turn of the pommel: in this exercise the centre of gravity of the weapon should move as little as possible.

For a right-hander, the *mulinello* done on the right hand side is termed a *mulinello externo* ("outside compass"), the *mulinello interno* ("inside compass") is done on your left-hand side. The *mulinelli* can go forwards or reverse, clockwise or anti-clockwise.

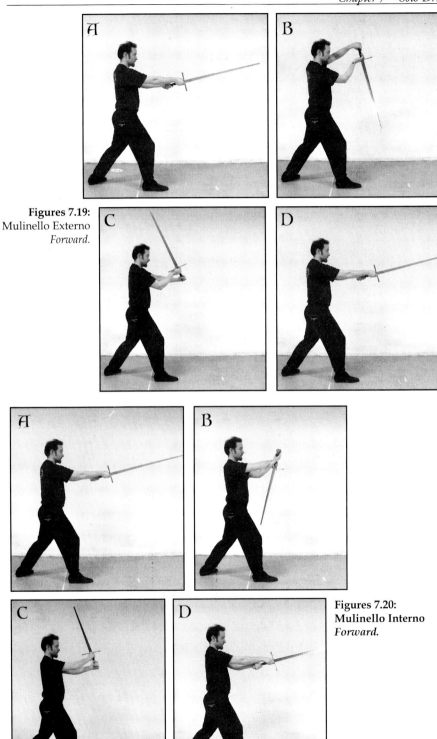

Figures 7.19:
Mulinello Externo
Forward.

Figures 7.20:
Mulinello Interno
Forward.

Figures 7.21:
Mulinello Externo
reverse.

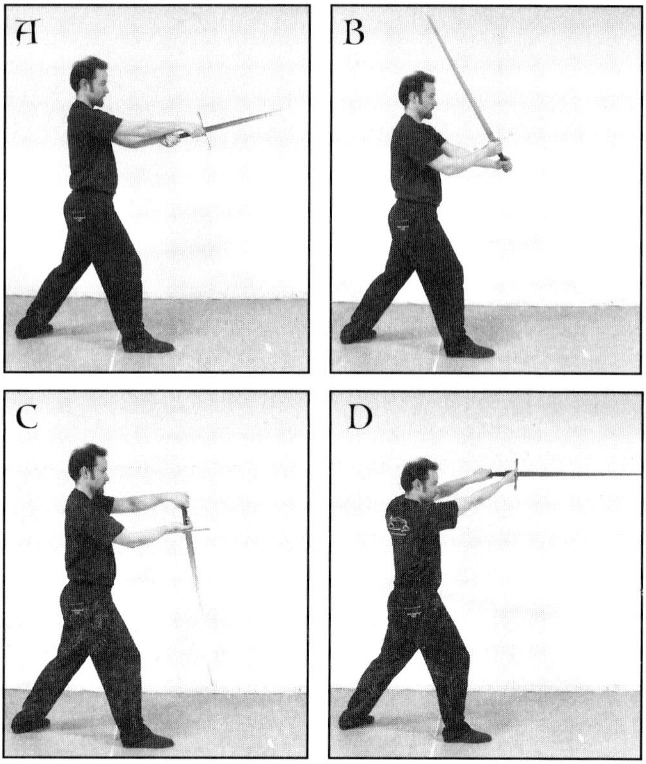

Figures 7.22:
Mulinello Interno
reverse.

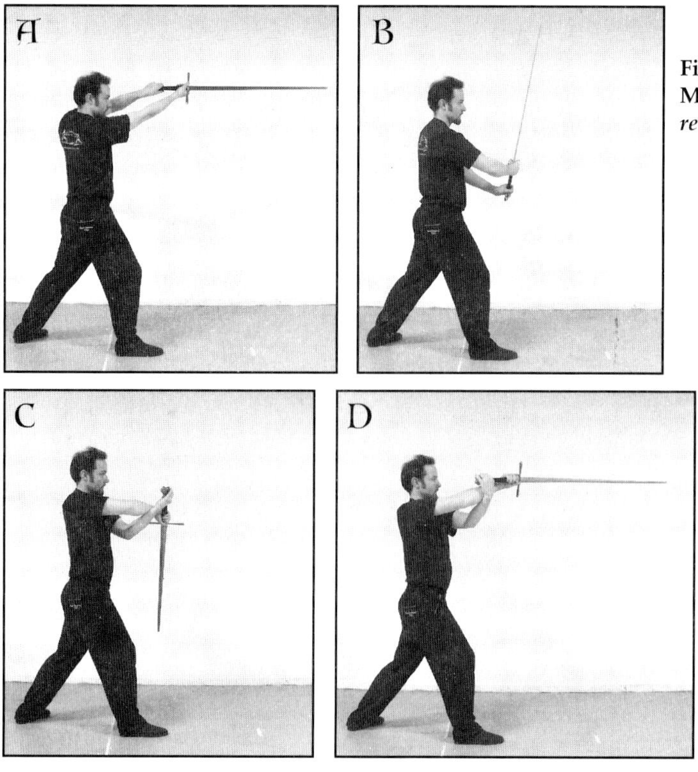

SHOULDER, ELBOW, AND WRIST CUTS

There are six main lines to cut through, and the cut may be driven by the shoulder, the elbow or the wrist. This exercise teaches you to be clear about the lines, and to distinguish between the three types of arm movement. Cuts from the shoulder that begin this exercise must be used carefully when fencing because they leave you open: a slight misjudgment of distance and you are very vulnerable. All cuts in this exercise are done with the **true** edge. The numbers refer to the numbering of the cuts in the SESH system.

1. Hold the sword in your right hand and assume *posta longa*. Keep the other hand behind your back.
2. Lift the weapon, with your arm almost straight, above your right shoulder.
3. Cut down *fendente mandritto* driving the cut from the shoulder, much like swinging an axe.
4. Keeping the arm extended, let the momentum carry the sword around in a *mulinello interno*, and cut down *fendente roverso*.
5. Turn the sword over so it is true-edge up, and through-cut *sottano mandritto*.
6. Allow the *sottano* cut to flow into a reverse *mulinello interno*, bringing the weapon around into a *sottano roverso*.
7. Let the point drop slightly so the sword is held horizontally over to your right, and cut across *mezano mandritto*.
8. Turn the sword over so the true-edge is to the right, and cut across *mezano roverso*.
9. Repeat steps 1-8, but allow the elbow to flex, doing most of the work. Keep the shoulder still, and the centre closed.
10. Repeat steps 1-8, but keep the elbow still, and do as much of the work as possible just with your wrist.
11. Repeat steps 1-10 with your left hand.
12. Repeat steps 1-11 with your normal two-handed grip.
13. Repeat the exercise but at steps 5 and 8 do not turn the hands: cut *mezano roverso* with the false edge instead.
14. It is also possible to do this exercise holding the sword with one hand by the pommel. This is an excellent strength training exercise, but be careful not to overstrain your wrists.

This exercise should be performed in a relaxed and easy manner, paying no attention to anything except the lines that you are cutting down, swinging the weapon smoothly through the correct angles.

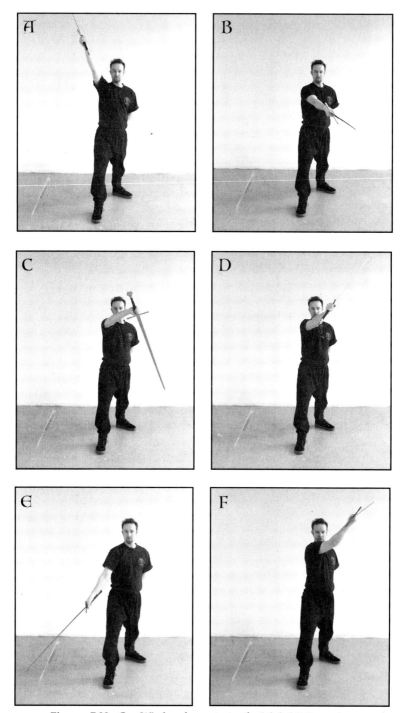

Figures 7.23: *Guy Windsor demonstrates the 1-2-3-4-5-6 exercise.*

(Continued from p. 96)

In the above exercise, notice that all *mulinelli* are *interno*, and all through-cuts are *mandritto*. The pattern should also be practised beginning with *fendente roverso* and ending with *mezano mandritto*, which allows you to practise *mulinelli externi*, and *roverso* through-cuts.

CUTTING EXERCISE **2,1,4,3,6,5**
1. Hold the sword in your right hand and assume *posta longa*. Keep the other hand behind your back.
2. Lift the weapon, with your arm almost straight, above your left shoulder.
3. Cut down *fendente roverso*, driving the cut from the shoulder.
4. Keeping the arm extended, let the momentum carry the sword around in a *mulinello externo*, and cut down *fendente mandritto*.
5. Turn the sword over so it is true-edge up, and cut up *sottano roverso*.
6. Allow the *sottano* cut to flow into a reverse *mulinello externo*, bringing the weapon around into a *sottano mandritto*.
7. Let the weapon drop slightly so the sword is held horizontally over to your left, and cut across *mezano roverso*.
8. Turn the sword over so the true-edge is to the right, and cut across *mezano mandritto*.
9. Repeat steps 1-8, but allow the elbow to flex, doing most of the work. Keep the shoulder still, and the centre closed.
10. Repeat steps 1-8, but keep the elbow still, and do as much of the work as possible just with your wrist.
11. Repeat steps 1-10 with your left hand.
12. Repeat steps 1-11 with your normal two-handed grip.
13. Repeat the above exercise but at steps 5 and 7 do not turn the hands: cut *sottano roverso* and *mezano roverso* withthe false edge instead.
14. If you do the previous sequence holding the sword with one hand by the pommel, also do it on this side. Again, be careful not to overstrain your wrists.

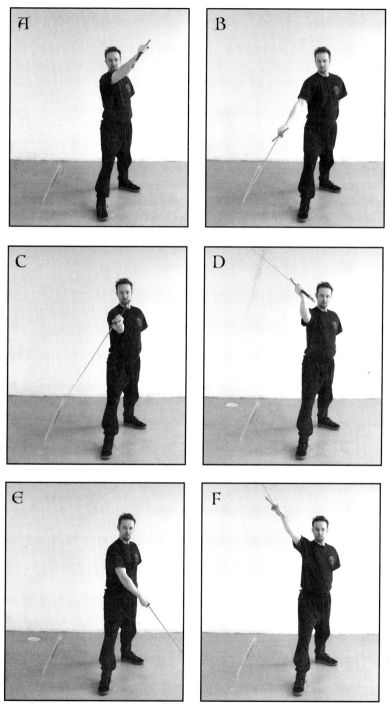

Figures 7.24: *Guy Windsor demonstrates the 2-1-4-3-6-5 exercise.*
(continuted p. 100)

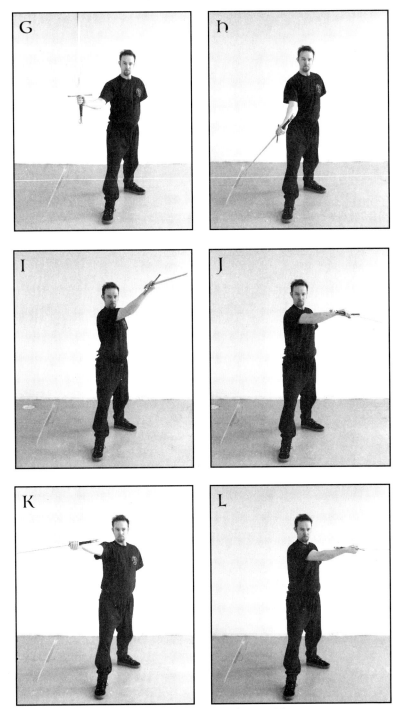

Figures 7.25 (continued from p. 99):
Guy Windsor demonstrates the 2-1-4-3-6-5 exercise.

Figures 7.26 :
A rendition of Filippo Vadi's version of
porta di ferro mezana
(see page 75).

DIAGONALS

This drill is used to develop the correct, relaxed and accurate method of driving the weapon with the handle.

CUTTING EXERCISE UP, DOWN, AROUND, AROUND

1. Begin in *posta longa*.
2. Lift the sword smoothly up the right diagonal, in the line of a *sottano roverso* until it is vertical.
3. Lower it down the same line. This should be done in a soft, wave-like way, slicing up with the back edge, and down with the true edge.
4. *Mulinello externo* forwards, cutting *fendente mandritto*, finishing in *posta longa*.
5. *Mulinello externo* reverse, cutting up *sottano mandritto*.
6. Repeat on the other side.

The whole exercise goes up, down, around, around; up down around, around. Imagine there is a paintbrush on the end of your sword: the line it draws on the wall would be a single stroke, from just above your right shoulder to about the centre of your chest. When repeated on the other side (*fendente roverso* etc.), the (imaginary) lines on the wall would form an X. Throughout the exercise your hands should remain above the waist, and pushing forwards. When cutting *sottano*, they should lift to just above eye height. Be very careful to follow the correct diagonal cutting angles, particularly with *sottani* cuts.

Figures 7.27:
Ville demonstrates stepping fendente *cut* mandritto.

Figures 7.28:
Ville demonstrates stepping fendente *cut* roverso.

LINEAR STEPPING

Having first mastered the footwork exercises, "stance stepping" is now used to power a cut.

1. Begin in *posta longa*, left foot forwards.
2. Contract back into *posta di fenestra*.
3. Push your weight forward, and your hands down and forward, into *posta breve*.
4. Push the hands forwards, step through with a pass, and lever-action the sword so the blade slices down *fendente mandritto*. At no time does the sword point behind you. The weapon does not go further back than the vertical.
5. Finish with the left hand below the right, both arms extended but not locked, in *posta longa*.
6. Contract back into *posta di fenestra*, right foot forwards, go through steps 3-5, cutting *fendente roverso*.
7. Repeat steps 2-6.

The points to remember are:
*   Remain relaxed. Power is not a product of tension.
*   Cut with your legs, and the lever, not by raising your arms.
*   Keep the weapon under total control at all times. Do not allow the point to fall below your solar plexus at any time during this exercise.
*   The weapon must remain in front of you at all times: do not allow it to point backwards.

Repeat the exercise. This time, at the point where the weapon is vertical, redirect the edge so that it cuts horizontally, *mezano mandritto* or *mezano roverso*. To begin with, the whole weapon should be parallel with the ground, and the cut aimed at heart height. Later, only the angle of the flat need remain horizontal: the point may rise or lower to cut as high as the neck, or as low as the knees: the hands remain at the same height.

To cut *sottano* from *posta di fenestra* or *posta breve*, you must use a reverse *mulinello*: at the moment when the sword is vertical, the point falls backwards in a circle behind you. It is vital that the angle of the cut is in the correct diagonal: too vertical and your wrists have to twist. Your hands must rise at the end of the cut to just above head height, with the weapon pushed as far forwards as possible.

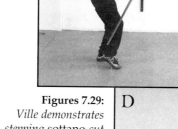

Figures 7.29:
Ville demonstrates stepping sottano *cut* mandritto.

Figures 7.30:
Ville demonstrates stepping sottano *cut* roverso.

Figures 7.31:
Ville demonstrates stepping mezano *cut* mandritto.

Figures 7.32:
Ville demonstrates stepping mezano *cut* roverso.

To cut *sottano* from *posta di fenestra* or *posta breve*, you must use a reverse *mulinello*: at the moment when the sword is vertical, the point falls backwards in a circle behind you. It is vital that the angle of the cut is in the correct diagonal: too vertical and your wrists have to twist. Your hands must rise at the end of the cut to just above head height, with the weapon pushed as far forwards as possible.

Of course, it would be suicidal to telegraph your intention in a fight by always contracting back to *fenestra* before cutting. Mastery of the above exercises will eventually allow you to feel how the weapon can be powered by a wave coming up from your feet. Then it becomes possible to cut in any angle from, for example, *posta breve*, without moving backwards at all. Instead, you can deliver a devastating cut with no apparent preparation.

CIRCULAR STEPPING

Cuts must also be practised with circular footwork: this delivers more power, but covers less distance. Beginning in *posta breve*, left foot forwards, step circularly forwards with the right foot, swinging around 135 degrees anticlockwise as described in "the ideal step". Allow that to power a *mandritto* cut in any of the three lines. Remember to lead with the weapon: though powered from the feet, the first thing to move is the sword. The edge hits the target at exactly the same time as your foot lands. Beginning with the right foot forwards you can circle forwards clockwise, and deliver a *roverso* in any line.

COMBINATION CUTTING

Having practiced stepping into the cut as in the last two exercises, combine cuts, particularly *sottano/fendente*. So step once, cut twice. Remember to keep your hands in the centre and as far forwards as possible. Use the lever of your handle to manipulate the blade: it should feel like the left hand is doing most of the work. Multiple cuts, rapidly executed, form the basis of most longsword attacks. Practise every possible pair combination of cuts, then multiple random cuts, in every line and with no designated number. Most fencers are not trained to deal with relentless attacks that come from all directions. (You soon will be. It's actually easy if you can keep your cool).

The majority of cutting problems may be solved by:
- Pushing the weapon forwards.
- Using the lever.
- Correcting your posture. Keep your head up and shoulders down.
- Concentrating on the correct lines.
- Timing the cut: the blade must hit the target at the same time as the foot touches the floor.

CONTROL

Control is the most obvious difference between an expert and a novice. It must be mastered on many levels. A swordsman should always be in control of himself, his emotions, and his tactical environment. Of course, a healthy human being must occasionally cede control (rigid, unyielding emotional sterility is not a requirement), and one must recognise that the world around us cannot be controlled. But in the Salle, in the street, and on the battlefield, self-control is all. The practice of swordsmanship over many years can and does lead to a measure of physical, mental and emotional self-control.

The body mechanics and footwork exercises are all about acquiring control over your body. The cutting practice is all about extending that control to your blade. **The golden, unbreakable rule of practice is that you *never* hit anyone either in anger or by accident.** Physical mastery of the basics leads to a devastating level of physical power: this must be balanced by equally highly developed physical and mental control.

Controlling your cuts is much less strenuous than most beginners seem to make it. It has practically nothing to do with the strength of your arms, and nothing at all to do with tensing up at the last moment. The total forward extension of the sword is determined by the extension of your right arm. The hand grips the sword just firmly enough, with the four fingers around the grip preventing the weapon from flying out and forwards. This means that left to itself, the pom- mel on the end of its long lever (the handle) comes back to- wards you. Your left arm, extended but not locked, positions the palm of your left hand as a stop. If you have practised the grounding exercises you are able to easily with- stand an adult pus-

hing with his entire weight against your hand: so it should be easy to prevent the pommel from coming too far back. Your left hand then can easily control the degree to which the sword is permitted to rotate forwards around the fulcrum of your right hand. The right hand determines how far forwards the fulcrum itself can go. The weapon is pulling against your right arm and pushing against your left: the forces are balanced and the rotation stops.

Because you always cut at full extension (though with the elbows soft, not locked), the total distance of your cut is determined by your feet. You must always come fully into distance when doing pair drills with your partner, so that if you chose, by allowing the hands to complete the rotation of the sword, you would hit the right place at the right time. The only difference between a cut that stops short of the target and a cut that goes through the target should be the degree of rotation of the sword around its centre.

It is a very good idea to practice at the pell doing full power cuts, stopping them with no muscular effort, just with the position of your bones. When cutting at the pell, you should push the limits of your control: in every 10 cuts, you should accidentally tap the wood 2 or 3 times. More than that and you are going too fast: less than that and you are not training at the limit of your control. As well as improving your cutting technique and control, the pell will give you a sense of how much power you can safely handle. Remember **when training with a partner you may not accidentally hit them even once in a *million* cuts.**

The Easy Way

There is a fast and easy way to learn to cut very hard with little effort. Simply transition back and forth between Fiore's *posta di donna* (right hand side) and *posta di dente cinghiale* (this gives you *fendente mandritto* and *sottano roverso*); and from *posta di donna* (left hand side) and *coda lunga distesa* (this gives you *fendente roverso* and *sottano mandritto*). However, this will teach only through-cuts, and nothing about control. In my system, I make the beginners learn the hard way (see the above exercises), then show this fast and easy method to the intermediates, who have by then acquired the control and tactical awareness to make appropriate use of it.

Thrusts

Every master of every type of sword who was kind enough to write down his system advocates the use of thrusts. Vadi describes them as "dangerous and quick; of all other (blows they are) Master." Fiore says they are "more poisonous than a snake."[10]

The advantages of the thrust are threefold: firstly, it does not require much power. Secondly, thrusts can stop someone in their tracks, particularly if the point stops on bone. Thirdly, they are easy to feint with, or change into from a cut.

As I see it, *thrusting* is the act of *pushing* your point through a vulnerable spot on your opponent. *Stabbing* is the act of *punching* your point through your opponent. In general, stab with short weapons, for speed, and thrust with long ones, for accuracy.

Thrusting Exercises

These exercises are designed to ensure that the mechanics supporting the thrust are correct. The forward component of the attack begins in the hands: it should feel like your sword is being pulled forward by the point. In each case (except with the Boar's thrust) if used defensively, the sword is used to simultaneously deflect an incoming attack; when used offensively, the sword closes your centre relative to your opponent's weapon. These actions will be done with a partner in the second *mezzo tempo* blade defence exercise; refer to the illustrations if you have trouble visualising the purpose of these exercises.

Boar's Thrust[11]

This thrust, beginning in *porta di ferro mezana* (or ideally in *posta di dente chinghiale* for those that know their Fiore) with the point rising from near the floor to solar-plexus height, is known as the Boar's thrust, and is supposed to enter the body just above the groin, ripping up and forwards until it hits the ribcage. Do not allow the point to rise too high.

Figures 7.33:
Miika Vanhapiha demonstrates the boar's thrust.

LATERAL OPPOSITION

From *posta breve*, left foot forward, sword on the right side of your body, thrust forward while stepping diagonally left. The sword travels straight forward, on the original line between your feet. The end position has your hands quite far out to your right side, and the sword angled forwards, approximately parallel to the ground. Repeat from the other side. The function here is for the weapon to maintain opposition to your imaginary opponent's attack, while your body evades.

VERTICAL OPPOSITION

This is the same as the second exercise, except that as your sword moves forward, the hilt rises to the *fenestra* position, then a little higher. The point travels forward into your opponent's face, angled slightly downwards. Done against a descending (*fendente*) cut, this will collect your opponent's weapon against your crossguard, controlling it while you thrust.

Figures 7.34:
Miika demonstrates the vertical opposition thrust, left side.

Figures 7.35:
Miika demonstrates the vertical opposition thrust, right side.

POINT CONTROL

This is the art of placing your point in exactly the right spot. The best-timed thrust, in perfect distance, will do nothing if it misses. It is therefore important that you practise your thrusts against a target. The longsword is usually too rigid to thrust with at a wall target (as with a rapier, for example). Instead, thrusts should be practiced on the pell, aiming to actually touch a given spot, in the correct line. A suitably reinforced punchbag also affords an excellent thrusting target.

Hilt Strikes

All parts of the longsword may be used offensively. When you find yourself too close to your opponent to use the blade, it is perfectly good practice to hit with whatever part of the weapon is convenient. Crossguard smashes to the throat and elbow occur in the treatises. It is also very effective to stab with the ends of the crossguard (Vadi recommends sharpening them for this purpose).

Strikes with the pommel[12] are particularly common, and occur repeatedly in both *Flos Duellatorum* and *De Arte Gladiatoria Dimicandi*.

The correct execution of a pommel strike allows you to get the full weight of the weapon and your body behind it. Keeping a firm grip on the sword, point it behind you and jab forwards with the pommel. This is usually done to the face, easily breaking the nose or teeth. Strikes under the point of the jaw, to the larynx and to the correct points on the skull can kill.

Figures 7.36: Giocco Stretto *from Fiore dei Liberi's Pissani-Dossi edition.*

A- *Novati 162/ carta 22B, fig. 1.*
B- *Novati 161/carta 22A fig. 3.*

CHAPTER 8

ARMED PRACTICE
PAIR DRILLS

T o understand the practical use of the longsword, it is necessary to cross swords with a partner, preferably one equally committed to proper training as yourself. As attacker or defender, you must retain a sense of emotional detachment from what you are doing: do not get carried away. Treat each exercise as an entirely academic activity. If you start to think about the exercise as defending yourself against a real attack, your body's instinctive defensive reflexes will kick in, and you will not be able to properly distinguish between the technique you are trying to do and your natural defence. Only when all the basic exercises are mastered, at speed, and you can choose at will from a whole range of defensive options, should you start to develop a more fight-realistic mindset. Nobody learns new technique in a fight.

If you are having trouble getting any particular technique right, slow down. It is perfectly correct and good training to practice technique at a speed that makes it look like you are wading through treacle. Speed is a product of good technique: speed is a result, not a goal. Speed comes from being able to execute any technique absolutely smoothly, in the right place at the right time.

The most annoying habit a student or training partner can possess is the tendency to counter the technique an instructor is showing them. The phrase "Ah, but I could do this!", will, in the end, force the instructor, a kind and patient individual most of the time, to demonstrate to said student that a) he doesn't know all the counters and b) there is a massive difference between knowing a possible counter, and being able to execute it at speed against a more experienced opponent. Every technique has a dozen counters. Do not waste time in the beginning getting sidetracked into working out ways to beat all the techniques you are supposed to be practicing: the counters will come in good time. For now, if an exercise requires you not to react, but to get "hit," the fact that your partner will attack slowly means that you will have time to flinch, block, counter, etc. Restrain yourself, or you will develop bad habits that will dog your later training. The purpose is to retrain your body with a new set of reactions that will work when the technique is done at speed. So stand your ground with *audatia*.

You must also respect the speed limit imposed by your level of control. When the exercises are working exactly as they should, then go a little faster. All the techniques below start with a very simple, obvious attack; the kind of thing that is unlikely to happen in free fencing. However, you need to stick to such clear actions to begin with, or you will never progress beyond really basic fencing. The chapter on free fencing will cover how and when to apply these techniques.

All instructions are given from the point of view of one fencer (usually the defender). So whenever it is written, for example, "step right", step to your right.

DWARVES, GIANTS AND LEFT-HANDERS

It is perfectly possible for a large right-hander and a small left-hander (or vice versa) to practise these techniques together. All the drills below work well with a pair of right-handers, a pair of left-handers, and a cross-handed[1] pair (one right handed, one left).

Figure 8.1: *Petri (195cm, 6'5", right-handed) and Piia (157.5cm, 5'2", left-handed).*

THE SALUTE

Before pairing off with your partner, and at the beginning and end of each training session, it is appropriate to salute. We have no way of knowing if this was advocated by the masters of this period, but the culture from which they sprung was built on precise hierarchies with precise codes of conduct. I don't know how it might have been performed during the fifteenth century, but for now, what matters is that it is clear, and executed with respect. The form we use at SESH is very simple.

1. Assume *posta porta di ferro*, right foot forwards.
2. Withdraw your front foot all the way back until it almost touches your back foot, while raising the crossguard to the level of your upper lip. The sword should be absolutely upright.
3. Hold it for a moment and catch the eye of your partner or opponent.
4. Lower your sword to your right side with the point almost on the ground.
5. Resume your guard position, or, if this marks the end of practice, step out normally.

The salute is a reminder that you are holding a deadly weapon, it helps to establish an appropriate mindset, and it serves to mark the beginning and end of each session.

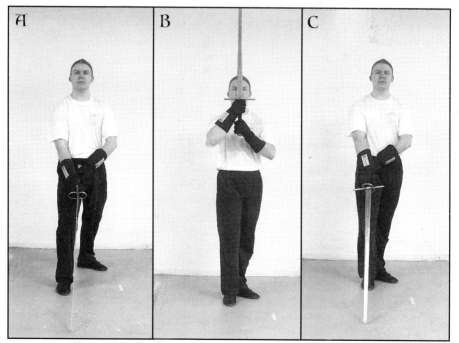

Figures 8.2: *Tanda Tuovinen demonstrates the salute used at SESH.*

Defences

Solo practice is the foundation of good technique, but foundations are only useful because they allow you to build upon them. The first function of swordsmanship practice is defence against attack.

There are three possible ways of defending yourself from a longsword attack:

- Counterattacking into the attack
- Parrying the attack
- Avoiding the attack

COUNTERATTACKS

This is without question the ideal defensive response in longsword fencing, emphasised in all Italian historical fencing styles. Longsword counterattacks are done in *mezzo tempo*. There are basically two ways of counterattacking in safety: with opposition and with avoidance. The counterattack with opposition is done by closing the line of your opponent's attack at the same time as you strike him. It is normal to avoid also when counterattacking with opposition; if your opposition fails, then the avoidance should save you. The counterattack with avoidance is usually directed at the advanced target (his hands): as he attacks, you get out of the way and chop his hands off. Again, if your counterattack fails, the avoidance should save you.

Parries

The term "parry" was probably imported into the English language from the Italian rapier masters working in London in the late sixteenth and early seventeenth centuries, and derives from the Italian verb *parere*, to set aside. With time, the term has come to mean any purely defensive blade action. Parries can be executed as either blocks or deflections.

Fiore's instructions regarding blade defence are very simple: against any attack, cross your blade with his. This is called the *incrosada*. This can be done as a collection of your opponent's weapon onto your crossguard, as a strike against the incoming sword, as a yielding deflection, or by cutting through. As a last-ditch defence, a block is also possible. Almost all of Fiore's longsword plays include an *incrosada* in some form.

BLOCKS

Against a cut, the most natural, reflexive action is what we call the "Oh Shit!" parry. The block is done edge on edge, and brings both weapons to a stop. As a last ditch defence, it is certainly better that getting hit, but it is not the best way of defending yourself.

DEFLECTIONS

A good swordsman can smash through a block. I doubt if any of my students could block a full-force blow from me, but the more experienced can certainly deflect even my most committed attack. In addition, hand-forged, expensive longsword blades need to be better looked-after than mass-produced sabre blades: they cost ten times as much. The best-forged blade in the world will still chip if bashed edge on edge with the worst.

The alternative, deflection, is similar to a block in that you use your blade to knock aside your opponent's. The difference lies in the fact that the deflection redirects the attacker's energy rather than stopping it. So while his blade is moving away from you, and yours is moving towards him, he has to reverse the momentum of his sword to effect a defence. This is much harder than recovering from a block. An experienced swordsman can use the energy of an oncoming attack to direct and power his own; equally, an experienced swordsman can use the energy of his opponent's deflection to redirect his attack, or to effect a defence. Remember that every technique has a counter; but some have more counters than others. Longsword *due tempi* defence is mostly concerned with the various types of deflection, immediately followed by a riposte.

Deflections can be made inside or outside the arc of the attack, with the sword point-up or point-down, with the true or false edge, and they can be done hard, as a sharp attack on the blade, softly so that your opponent has very little awareness of the deflection, "stickily" to retain contact with the blade, or as a push to expel the blade. In practice, there are four types of deflection:

1. **Impulse**: the incoming blade is easily sent off-course with a sharp strike. You may use the impulse to springboard your riposte off his blade.
2. **Cutting through**: by cutting through the opposing line, it is possible to smash through the incoming attack. Against a diagonal cut (*fendente* or *sottano*) you can cut up or down the opposite diagonal, or across with *mezano* to deflect. For example, if the incoming attack is travelling down from your left to your right, a rising cut from your left to your right, or a descending cut from your right to your left, aimed at the incoming blade, will knock it away. *Mezano* attacks can also be dealt with this way, and *mezano* can be used defensively this way.
3. **Collection**: by making contact with the incoming blade with your own, you can direct it to your crossguard. From there you can easily control his weapon.
4. **Yielding**: Making contact with the incoming blade but not opposing it, instead allowing it to blow through your position, seems suicidal. However, done correctly with either *frontale* or *fenestra* it is very safe, allowing you to "steal" the energy of the attack and use it to power your defense.

The purpose of a deflection is to close the line of the attack and to gain momentary control over your opponent's blade. This is effected by degree and by opposing your edge to their flat.

DEGREE

This describes the position of the point of contact between the two blades, relative to the hilts. Most *incrosada* are executed at the middle of the swords: you aim for the contact to be at the middle of his blade, and at the middle of yours (Vadi refers to this as *mezza spada*, "half sword"). This is because you must protect your fingers: longswords do not come with knucklebows.

To control your opponent's weapon, you need a lever; so you want the connection to be as close to your hilt as possible, and as close to his point as possible. This effectively provides you with the longest possible lever with which to move his sword wherever you want it to go. To acquire this kind of contact (as is shown repeatedly in *Fior di Battaglia*) it is first necessary to make an *incrosada* at *mezza spada*, then allow your opponent's blade to slide down towards your hilt.

EDGE TO FLAT

If you are holding your sword correctly, then your edge is supported by your forearm: pressure against your edge can be easily withstood. However, pressure against the flat of the blade exerts a twisting force on your arm which cannot be easily resisted. In addition, the sword itself is easily bent across the flat, but practically impossible to bend in line with the edges. Try this by positioning your partner in *posta longa*, holding the true edge of his sword with your hand, and leaning your weight against it. He should be able to resist quite easily. Then, using only one finger against the flat of his blade about four inches from the point, move his weapon across: he will not be able to resist (unless he switches his grip, and even then the sword will bend and the pressure against the thumb becomes intolerable).

Figure 8.3: *Demo, edge vs. flat*

It should therefore be obvious that whenever possible you should oppose your strength, the edge, to his weakness, the flat, when making deflections.

There has been some disagreement in historical fencing circles as the whether you may parry with edge or flat. This disagreement, as far as I can tell, derives from an insufficiently precise use of the terms "parry," and "flat." It is demonstrably impossible to block a cut with the flat of your sword.

It is occasionally possible to use a beat with the flat, against the flat of the incoming sword, to set aside the attack. Most deflections are done with the edge of the defender's sword against the flat of the attacker's, but given the relative angles of attack, it is quite common for the deflection to appear to be done with the flat against the edge. In the case of a false-edge inside deflection against a *mandritto roverso*, for example, if the weapons were static, the attacker's edge would find your flat; but because the deflection is effectively cutting backwards, you are in fact cutting at the attacker's sword, meeting it in such a way that your edge finds their flat. The "flat" of a sword is very rarely actually flat: common cross-sections include diamond, oval, and concave-fullered flats. In this case, your edge is making contact with the part of the blade that is tapering towards the edge (the "bevel").

Hilt Parries

The crossguard of the longsword can and should be used to catch your opponent's attack. This is done by making an *incrosada* at *mezza spada*, using *posta frontale* or *posta di fenestra*; your blade directs the incoming blade your crossguard. Once this trap is effected, it is easy to control your opponent's weapon.

Avoidance

A cardinal principle of defence is to be where the attack is not. If you are not there, he can't hit you. The principle of avoidance works on two levels: firstly, do not get into a fight. This is perhaps the most important aspect of martial arts training: if you have to use it for real, you have already made some serious mistakes. Just as a doctor should ideally spot a disease and cure it in the very early stages, long before the patient's life is threatened, so a martial artist should spot the potential for a fight and avoid it long before the first blow is struck. Secondly, if your avoidance has failed at the first level, or you are just practising, then use body avoidance (such as a sidestep) to avoid specific attacks. In training we practice avoidance of the attack simultaneously with deflections. Generally speaking, your defence should always be two-fold, so if one aspect fails, the other will cover you.

Avoidance is done to the inside or the outside of your opponent's attack. The best place to be in a fight is usually behind your opponent. To get there you have to go outside his attack. If he is in the process of attacking you with, for example, a *fendente mandritto*, then the shortest route to get behind him is to the left, through his cut. This presents practical difficulties related to having your head cut off, so before you move to his outside, you must first clear the way. A sword in motion is, as the exercises below will show you, very easily knocked off-course. It is perfectly possible to knock his weapon up and across, using a through-cutting deflection. This action is made safer if you keep your crossguard between his blade and your head: if his blade slides down yours, if your hands are far enough forwards, and high enough, his blade can't hit you.

Avoidance to the inside is also effective, but leaves the attacker with more options as you remain in front of him. The general rule regarding avoidance is this: *always step away from the blade contact*. So if you are defending on the inside against a *mandritto* attack to your left side, step to the right. When executing an outside deflection, defending against the same attack you would step to the left. This becomes obvious the first time you walk into your opponent's blade.

Counters to Defences

There are three ways of countering a counterattack:

- **Opposition**: as your attack is made, close the line of his counterattack and push through.
- **Avoidance**: if his counterattack is done in such a way that you cannot close the line, it may be possible to get out of the way.
- **Deception**: if you can draw out the counterattack against a provocation you have made, it is possible to oppose, deflect, avoid, or re-counter, as against any attack.

There are three ways of countering a block or deflection:

- **Deceive it**: by changing the line of your attack before your opponent's blade touches yours (as in false play).
- **Yield to it**: allow the deflection to redirect your blade, but not your hilt, keeping your centre closed.
- **Deal with his riposte** (his attack after his successful deflection), with any of the defences you know (avoidance, deflection, counterattack).

There are three ways of countering avoidance:

- **Follow it**: as your opponent steps to the side or back, follow him.
- **Deception**: induce your opponent to sidestep, and change line so that he walks into your attack.
- **Close in**: once you have a grip on some part of him (usually the sword arm) with your left hand, it is much easier to anticipate, prevent or counter any subsequent avoidance.

The basic rule of all fencing technique is this: *close your centre, attack his centre.* This is achieved by keeping your sword (blade, cross or pommel) moving towards his centre and keeping your sword between his sword and your centre. All techniques and all tactics are essentially ways of executing this rule in practice.

Attack and Defence Are One

This is a rather gnomic way of saying that a true defence always contains within it an actual or potential attack; a true attack must always be executed defensively. It is foolish fencing to attack without defence, and suicidal to defend without attack. Remembering that you must always close the centre and attack, in practice it should make little difference whether you are attacking on your own initiative, or responding to your opponent's attack. The effect and the likely techniques are the same.

SQUARING OFF

> *Climb if you will, but remember that courage and strength are nothing without prudence, and that a momentary negligence may destroy the happiness of a lifetime. Do nothing in haste; look well to each step; and from the beginning think what may be the end.*[5]

Edward Whymper's admonition from *Scrambles amongst the Alps* elegantly encapsulates the correct attitude to all potentially lethal activities. Substitute "practice swordsmanship" for "climb," and there is the correct mindset for any fencer, beginner or expert. Take it to heart before you start training with a partner.

BLADE DEFENCE/ PAIR PRACTICE PREPARATION
All cuts must be executed in the correct distance, and controlled as detailed in the "Control" section. To recap, you must execute your cut while stepping completely into range, stopping it by controlling the rotation of the sword. Do not waste time by practising out of range. If you are wearing protection (as you should be) you can practise to a light touch on the mask. Repeated over-zealous taps on the mask can give you a headache, or worse. Touch as you mean to get touched, and if in doubt, be more gentle. If you have not got a mask yet, get one. In the meantime, it is vital to establish a safety zone around your partner. The safety zone is shown in the figure (right):

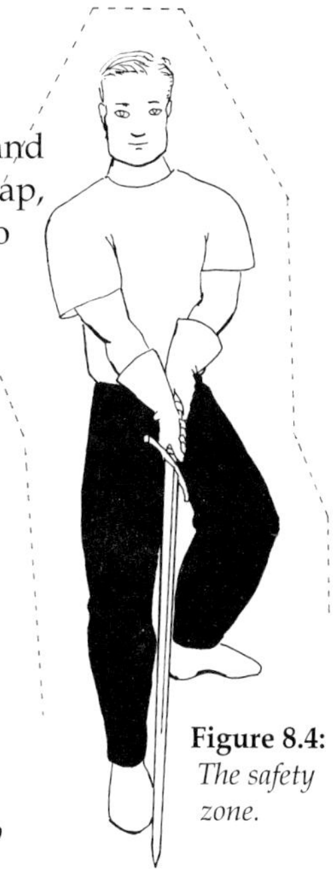

All the pair exercises begin with you and your partner in correct cutting distance.

Figure 8.4: *The safety zone.*

To find your correct distance:
1. Your partner stands on guard in *porta di ferro mezana*.
2. Approach your partner with your sword extended (*posta longa*), and place it in the air above his left shoulder, as if you were cutting *fendente mandritto*. Be sure that your position is correct (back straight, right foot forwards, arms extended), and that you are in exactly the right distance to hit him with the correct part of the blade.
3. Leaving your left foot exactly where it is, pivoting it as necessary, step back with the right foot and take up either *posta breve* or *posta di fenestra*.
4. Cut *fendente mandritto*. Check that it is in the correct line, aimed at the junction of neck and shoulder, and that if you were to complete the cut, you would hit with the correct part of the blade.
5. Step back as in step 3.

You are now sure of distance and are ready to begin the exercises. It is important that any necessary adjustments to the distance be made by the attacker: if the defender shuffles around trying to help, the attacker will never learn their own range.

Giocco Largo Defences
MEZZO TEMPO BLADE DEFENCE EXERCISES

1. COUNTERATTACKS WITH THE EDGE:

To the advanced target:
Against direct attacks, you can sidestep a little further away, out of range of his attack, and cut at his wrists or fingers, normally with a *fendente* or *sottano* cut. A good example of this is the false edge *sottano* done against a *fendente*.

1. Begin in *porta di ferro mezana*
2. Partner cuts *fendente mandritto*.
3. Sidestep to the right, lifting your false edge up in the line of *sottano roverso*, cutting up at his wrists.

This can also be done over the top, with a *fendente* cut.

To the main target
1. Begin in *porta di ferro mezana*
2. Partner cuts *fendente mandritto*
3. Sidestep forwards and to the right, cutting *fendente mandritto*. Your *forte* should collect his blade while the cut touches his mask.

Figure 8.5: *Cuts und and over the hands.*
B- A cut under the hands.
C- A cut over the han

It is possible to counterattack with *fendente*, *mezano*, or *sottano* against a cut in any line: work through the possible combinations with your partner to discover which ones work best for you.

Figure 8.6:
A countercut to the head.

2. COUNTERATTACKS WITH THE POINT: OPPOSITION THRUSTS

Refer to the thrusting exercises before attempting this pair drill. One of the most stylish counterattacks is the *thrust with opposition*.

1. Begin in *porta di ferro mezana*.
2. Partner cuts *sottano mandritto*.
3. Cut *sottano mandritto*, pushing your point forwards towards his belly, with the *forte* of your true edge pushed out to the left, collecting his blade as you go. Your weapon will slope down at about 30 degrees, with the cross and flat parallel to the ground. This is adapted from the lateral opposition thrust exercise.

This is a very simple, easy technique if you trust it. Make sure that you oppose his blade properly, but do not let your sword travel too far out to the side. The main purpose of the action is the thrust forwards. Now repeat 1-3 with a sidestep to the right, stepping just after your sword has started to move forwards. Repeat this exercise against *sottano roverso*, pushing the true edge over to the right, and stepping to the left. Repeat this exercise against *fendenti* cuts, using the vertical opposition thrust, aimed at the face. Against *mezani* cuts, again thrust at the face, but with the hands just below (if the cut is to your head) or above his blade (if the cut is aimed lower), and opposing laterally.

Figures 8.7:
Opposition thrust against
sottano, mezano *and*
fendente *cuts.*
A- *Against a* Sottano
B- *Against a* Fendente

Figures 8.7:
C- Against a Fendente Roverso.
D- Against a Mezano.

Figures 8.7 (continued):
*E- Against a Mezano Rov-
erso.*

DUE TEMPI BLADE DEFENCE EXERCISES.

Impulses
Impulses are perhaps the most commonly used, easiest and natural blade defence. The deflection must close your centre relative to the line of attack, and without stopping become an attack.

1. Begin in *porta di ferro mezana*.
2. Partner cuts *fendente mandritto*.
3. Lever your sword up into *posta frontale*, directing your true edge against the incoming sword at *mezza spada* with a sharp strike to his blade.
4. Springboard your blade off his, and deliver a properly controlled *fendente mandritto*.

It is very important that you do not look for his blade: if it isn't there yet you can't hit it. Time your action to his so that you are striking his blade near the end of his attack. Too late and you get hit, too early and you get hit. Do this technique exactly as if you were just cutting to the air. Repeat this exercise against *fendente* and *mezani* attacks on both sides (*mandritto* and *roverso*). When you are comfortable with this technique, try also using the false edge to deflect. It requires a slight turn of the hands to direct the edge cleanly against the incoming blade.

You should find that point-up deflections are most easily done with the true edge on your inside line (against his *fendente mandritto*), and with the false edge on your outside line (against his *fendente roverso*). In general this is how they should be done when fencing, but it is worth practising them both ways as a technical study.

Figures 8.8:
Against Miika's fendente mandritto, *Ville executes a true edge impulse and ripostes.*

Figures 8.9:
Against Rami's fendente
roverso, *Nikodemus executes
a false edge impulse and
ripostes.*

CUTTING THROUGH

A firmer and more vigorous deflection than the impulse can be executed by cutting through the incoming attack. Simply traverse your sword in a normal cut through the opposing line, aiming to hit the icoming sword at *mezza spada*.

Part one – *sottano*, false edge:
1. Begin in *porta di ferro mezana*.
2. Partner cuts *fendente mandritto*.
3. Using the lever action, direct your point under the incoming blade and beat it sharply with your false edge against his flat. Your hands will have to traverse up and across to the right to be sure of directing his blade up and over. Be very careful. This action is a *sottano roverso*.
4. Continue the lever action without pause to execute a fendente mandritto cut to the correct target.

Figures 8.10:
As Miika attacks fendente roverso, *Jari sidesteps and cuts up* sottano mandritto *with his false edge, deflecting Miika's cut, and continues with* fendente roverso.

Repeat this action against *fendente roverso*, making sure to traverse your hands across to the left somewhat during step 3 (*sottano mandritto*).

Part two - *sottano*, true edge:

The reverse *mulinello* can also be used defensively:

1. Begin in *porta di ferro mezana*.
2. Partner cuts *fendente mandritto*.
3. Using the through-cutting action, direct your point under the incoming blade, and cutting upwards *sottano roverso*, beat it sharply with your true edge against his flat. Your hands will have to traverse up and across to the right to be sure of directing his blade up and over. Again, be very careful.
4. Continue the through-cutting action without pause to execute a *fendente mandritto* cut to the correct target.

Repeat this action against *fendente roverso*, making sure to traverse your hands across to the left somewhat during step 3.

When you can reliably execute the outside deflections, sidestep simultaneously with the deflection as described above. Be certain to step correctly so that you are moving away from the blade contact, and finishing in a position in which you are directing yourself and your weapon clearly in the shortest line to the target. Against his *mandritto*, step left, against *roverso*, step right.

You may have noticed that the action of cutting sottano with the false edge has you transitioning through *posta longa*; and when cutting up with the true edge, you finish the cut in *fenestra*. It is important to AIM your cut at the midpoint of the incoming blade.

Figures 8.11:
True edge cut through against a fendente mandritto.

Part three – *fendente*, true edge:
1. Begin in *posta di donna* on the right.
2. Partner cuts *fendente mandritto*.
3. Using the through-cutting action, cut down *fendente mandritto* through the incoming blade, while sidestepping diagonally right with your right foot. This takes you to *dente di chinghiale*.
4. Thrust immediately to the belly (heading into *posta longa*).

Repeat this exercise against *fendente, mezani* and *sottani* attacks on both sides (*mandritto* and *roverso*).

COLLECTIONS

Using *Frontale*
An alternative to an impulse deflection is to shift into *frontale*: do not get rid of their blade, but allow it to travel to the crossguard. From there you may strike with edge or point, grasp their blade, enter into *giocco stretto*, etc. Most of Fiore's longsword plays can be done from this position.

1. Begin in *porta di ferro mezana*.
2. Partner cuts *fendente mandritto*.
3. Lift your sword into *posta di frontale*, intercepting his blade at *mezza spada*, and directing it to your crossguard.

Figure 8.12:
Ilkka (right) prepares to attack Antti with **fendente mandritto**.
(continued next page)

133

Figures 8.12b:
Ilkka attacks: Antti lifts his sword into **posta frontale** *and meets him* **mezza spada**.

Figures 8.12c:
Ilkka's blade slides down to Antti's crossguard.

Figures 8.12d & e:
D- Ikka has attacked roverso;
Antto collects him at mezza
spada
*E- ...and his blade slides down
to Antti's crossguard.*

Using Fenestra

This action is almost invariably done to the outside, and can finish with a cut, a thrust or a disarm.

1. Begin in *porta di ferro mezana*.
2. Partner cuts *fendente mandritto*.
3. Step forwards and to the left with your left foot, bringing your sword up to *fenestra* on your right, making contact with the incoming blade and letting it slide down to your crossguard.

Figures 8.13:
Posta fenestra *collection to the outside.*

Figures 8.13 (continued): *Details on the* fenestra *collection to the outside.*

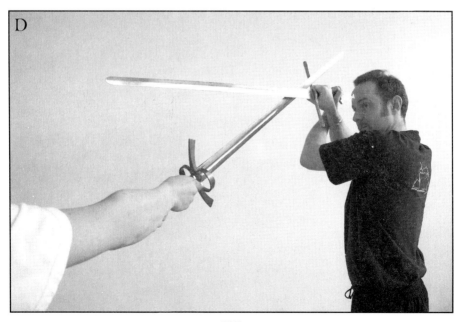

YIELDING

A yielding deflction does not stop the incoming sword; the attacker should feel that the defender's attack is continuing through. However, there is enough resistance in your weapon's position that the attack slides away from you. Yielding deflections are done either with *fenestra* or *frontale*.

Posta di Fenestra to the inside:
1. Begin in *porta di ferro mezana.*
2. Partner cuts *fendente mandritto.*
3. Step to the right with your right foot, and raise your weapon so that the blade is horizontal and your right hand is by your right temple. This is simply *posta di fenestra* on the right. At the moment that your blade intercepts his, the contact is in the middle of the blade.

Figure 8.14:
Fenestra done to the outside. Antti has attacked mandritto, *I deflected with a left-side* fenestra.

Figures 8.15:
A- *Antti prepares to attack Ilkka with a* mandritto.
B- *As Antti attacks, Ilkka sidesteps right (inside the cut) into* posta di fenestra, *meeting Antti's sword* mezza spada.
C- *Antti's attack blows through, sending Ilkka's sword around and into a* fendente mandritto. *Ilkka's left foot has followed him around to support the cut and complete the avoidance.*

Figures 8.16:
A- Antti prepares to attack with a roverso.
B- Ilkka sidesteps left into posta di fenestra, *inside Antti's cut, and...*
C- ...yields to it, sending his sword around into a fendente roverso. Ilkka's right foot follows the action.

Try to keep the weapon moving smoothly from the moment your hands start to rise to the moment that your cut is finished. You can direct your cut *fendente mandritto* as above, in which case the sword rotates in a flat circle, or you can counter with *fendente roverso*, in which case the sword describes a cone in the air.

Repeat this exercise against *roverso* attacks; it is then necessary step to the left, and take *fenestra* on the left.

The classic mistake here is to intercept his blade with your fingers: keep to *fenestra*, and your hands are safe. In the course of my researches it took two cracked knuckles and one broken finger before I figured this out.

With practice, and with protection, you should be able to absorb the energy of the attack into your blade, letting it power your weapon around. If your grip is soft and you do not resist the attack, you can allow the attack to blow through; your sword directs his blade away from your sufficiently that you are safe. As he blows through, he will push your blade down: use that momentum to power your cut. Given the point of contact (*mezza spada*) you do not have the leverage to really resist the attack; so just redirect it.

Fenestra to the outside

Once you have the hang of cutting up under the incoming blade, it should become clear that you can step into *fenestra* to the outside of the cut.

Against a *mandritto* cut, stepping to the outside of the cut into *fenestra* on the left gives you a yielding deflection, to be followed with a *fendente* cut. As you saw in the Collection exercise, stepping into *fenestra* on the right instead would give you a blade collection and a thrust to his face (see fig. p. 138).

Getting to the outside with *Frontale*

This is the one time that you will actually step towards blade contact.

1. Begin in *porta di ferro mezana*.
2. Partner cuts *fendente mandritto*.
3. Step forwards and slightly to the left with your front (right) foot, raising your sword into *frontale*.
4. As the blades make contact at *mezza spada*, allow your blade to be pushed over to the right, but keep your hilt high. Your partner's weapon should push yours over until it is pommel-forwards.
5. Pass through with your left foot to strike with the pommel (this is the most natural continuation from here).

Figures 8.17:
A- Ilkka prepares to attack Guy with a roverso.
B- As Ilkka attacks, Guy steps a little left and meet's his blade in posta frontale *at* mezza spada.

Figures 8.17 (continued):
C- Ilkka's cut pushes Guy's blade over towards fenestra.
D- Guy steps in to shoulder distance and pushes Ilkka's chin.
E- Ilkka having attacked roverso, *Guy met him in* frontale *as before; Ilkka's cut has pushed Guy's cut again into* fenestra...
F- ...Guy now steps in and strikes with the pommel.

Counters to Counterattacks

The primary defence against a counterattack with edge or point into your attack is to *reacquire opposition*. Part of the ability to do this lies in distinguishing between circular and linear body movement. In effect, you must perceive the counterattack as it is done, and turn your body into it, pushing your attack through.

Countering a counterattack to the main target exercise:
1. Begin in *posta di fenestra*, left foot forwards.
2. Partner assumes *porta di ferro*.
3. Attack *fendente mandritto*.
4. Partner sidesteps forwards and to his right, cutting *fendente mandritto*. His *forte* should collect your blade.
5. At or just before the moment of contact, turn your hips anticlockwise and push your hands towards his face. Your cut should touch his mask. If you find that you are out of range to cut, then thrust.

Repeat this exercise with all six cuts, and against counterattacks with the point. It will work, but will require subtle modifications that are beyond the scope of this book to describe. With enough practice, you will develop sufficiently sensitive *sentimento di ferro* to execute these techniques effortlessly.

Tactically, the above technique is used to tempt an opponent out of a passive guard. Imagine your opponent is in *coda lunga distesa*. You know that if you attack, he is ready to counterattack, probably with a *fendente* or *sottano*. If your first attack is completely committed, it will be very difficult to defend against his counterattack. Likewise, if you just feint, he may not be convinced by the feint, or may counterattack into it with sufficient resolution to prevent your second action. So, make your attack slightly short; this will give you fractionally more time to reacquire opposition, and will make your attack safer because his counterattack is also likely to be slightly out of distance. This is a good example of second intention. As an exercise, it would look like this:

Figure 8.18:
A- Guy (right) prepares to attack Ville with a fendente roverso.

1. False-attack *fendente mandritto*, stepping in but slightly out of reach. Your arms must extend fully for your attack to be convincing.
2. Partner sidesteps to his right, cutting *fendente mandritto*. His *forte* should collect your blade. Because you are slightly further away than anticipated, he will be just out of range, or will have to sidestep slightly closer, which takes longer.
3. At or just before the moment of contact, turn your hips anticlockwise and push your hands towards his face. Your cut should touch his mask. If you find that you are out of range to cut, then thrust. This works because you have set it up: you *wanted* him to counterattack.

Figure 8.18:
B- *Guy attacks; Ville steps in counterattacking with a fendente mandritto to Guy's head...*
C- *...Guy pivots his hips and pushes through Ville's cut, gaining his head. Note the collection of Ville's sword, and the change in Guy's body position.*

Countering a counterattack to the forward target exercise:

1. Attack *fendente mandritto*.
2. Partner sidesteps forwards and to his right, cutting up at your hands *sottano roverso*.
3. Catch his cut on your crossguard (use *posta frontale*), while turning to follow his evasion, and continue your attack.
4. Repeat, attacking with all six cuts, and with your partner counterattacking over your hands (*fendente*).

Figures 8.19:
A- Guy attacks; Tanda sidesteps and cuts up at his hands.

B- In response, Guy drops his hands to collect Tanda's blade (from here he can strike, or enter into giocco stretto*).*

Figures 8.19: (continued)
C- Guy has again attacked, and Tanda now cuts over his hands.

D- Guy collects the sword at posta frontale, *and from here can enter into* giocco stretto *or strike as before.*

1. Yielding to the Deflection

Resisting a deflection would require you to oppose strength (his edge) with weakness (your flat); clearly a bad idea. Equally, giving up control of your weapon to your opponent is not good. When you cut either *fendente* or *mezano*, the deflection that occurs in the above exercises imparts an impulse to your blade. Let the blade go, but keep your sword-hand in place, and a natural *posta di fenestra* point-down deflection will occur. This should quite easily catch your opponent's counter strike. This works because it does not rely on reaction time, but in effect, your opponent is pushing your weapon in front him: all you have to do is keep your centre closed and he will do the rest.

The illustration below shows this phenomenon occurring when a *fendente mandritto* is deflected upwards from the outside, and again when deflected on the inside.

Now practise this action as a counter to all the above drills. You will notice that it does not work against a yielding deflection, because you cannot yield: he is not imparting energy to the blade. You must then use either a deception (see below), or deal with his riposte with a deflection or counterattack. If you are having difficulty with this exercise, remember always to push your hands forward towards your opponent: your cut should flow around his defence, your hands always seeking to dominate the centre.

The practice of yielding to superior force effectively gives you another means of attacking: when your partner strikes your blade to deflect your attack, you can also use that energy to simply redirect your attack to the other side. This is most easily done against a *cut through*.

Figures 8.20 (continues on p. 150):
A- Rani (left) prepares to attack Nikodemus.
B- Rami now attacks while Nikodemus executes a true-edge through-cut deflection to the outside, simultaneously sidestepping under Rami's blade...

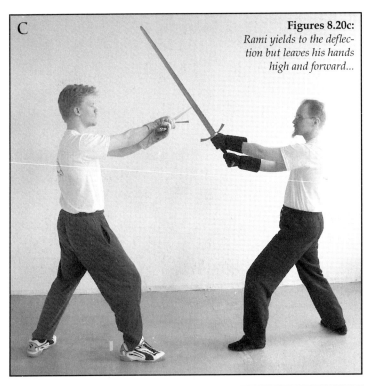

Figures 8.20c:
Rami yields to the deflection but leaves his hands high and forward...

Figures 8.20d:
...deflecting Nikodemus' attack with fenestra to the inside, which presses Rami's blade downward.

Figures 8.20 (continued):

E- Rami has this time attacked roverso, Nikodemus delfects to the outside as before...
F- Rami yields to the deflection and effects his own deflection to Nikodemus' riposte.
G- Rami finishes with a cut to the head, while Nikodemus tries without luck to deflect the strike.

2. Successive Attacks / Deception / Compound Attacks

A firm and vigorous attack, executed defensively (a paradox at the heart of good swordsmanship) should leave no room for your opponent's defence. This does not mean that you should flail away like an idiot, nor that you should lose control.

Successive attacks are, as the name implies, any series of cuts or thrusts, each intended to hit the target, and each parried or avoided. Deception in this context is the art of convincing your opponent that you are about to do one action, to draw his response, which you then avoid to create the opportunity for your attack. A compound attack, as opposed to successive attacks, is an attack that contains one or more feints; the feint being an attacking action intended to force a parry which will be deceived.

At an advanced level, your opponent will be able to sense which attacks are real, and which merely feints. This makes feinting useless except against relative beginners, until you are trained enough to be able to convert a feint into a real attack. So, in each of the following exercises, execute both attacks to the target. Your partner should only attempt the deflection every now and then. When he does, avoid it (do not allow any blade contact), and execute your real attack. If the deflection is successful, (because it is properly executed and you fail to avoid it) your partner should continue his action and riposte.

All compound attacks are done with changes of line. Remember that the target is divided into four quadrants, high inside, high outside, low inside and low outside. Because any parry can only cover one line at a time, the idea is to feint into an open line, to force your opponent to close that line with a parry, and then redirect your attack into a line that is being opened by his movement. The three main combinations are (see figures 8.21-8.23 p. 153-155):

- High-low: the first attack is done with *fendente*, the second *sottano* or *mezano*. This can be reversed, to become a low-high.
- Right-left (*mandritto-roverso*): in this action, the attack changes side. This is particularly commonly used against a fencer who gives ground, but can also be used very effectively to deceive his deflections. It can of course be done in reverse, as *roverso-mandritto*. It is quite common to combine these two methods, to create, for example, a high *mandritto* followed by a low *roverso* multiple attack.
- Cut-thrust: in this action, the cut (in whichever line) is converted into a thrust. This is usually done by pulling your weapon straight back, to get the point inside the deflection. It is also possible to dip the point under your opponent's blade, or (if he has tried a point down deflection) to lift it over his hands. A thrust may be followed by a cut, but the only cut available to you directly from the thrust is the draw-cut, which is not terribly powerful (though may be lethal when done to the right target, such as the throat), so one normally only follows a thrust with a cut if the thrust misses, and you bring the weapon back doing damage on the way.

Figures 8.21:
A- *Ville ready to attack Zoë*
Chandler.
B- *Ville attacks* fendente
mandritto. *Zoë attempts and*
inside true edge deflection.
C- Before the blades meet,
Ville avoids Zoë's parry, and
redirects his attack into the
line of fendente sottano
(high-low).

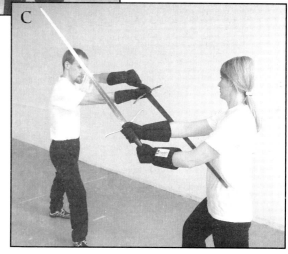

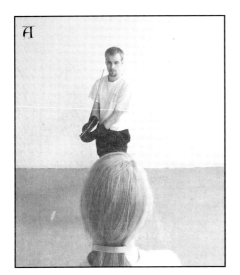
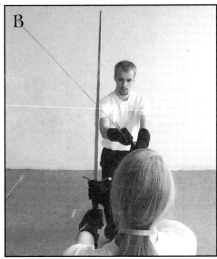
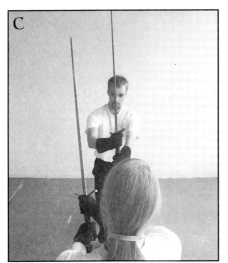
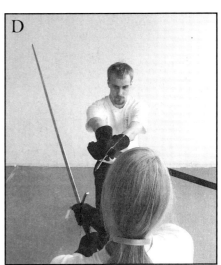

Figures 8.22:
A-*Ville ready to attack Zoë.*
B- *Ville attack fendente mandritto. Zoë attempts and inside true edge deflection.*
C,D- *before the blades meet, Ville avoids Zoë's parry, and redirects his attack to the line of* fendente roverso *(right-left).*

Figures 8.23:
A- Zoë ready to attack Nikodemus.
B- Zoë attacks fendente mandritto, Nikodemus attempts to parry with a point down deflection.
C- Before the blades touch, Zoë pulls her hands back and thrusts (cut-thrust).

By now you should, through diligent practise of the above exercises, have a fair idea about how the longsword works: the drill below should be attempted from all lines of attack, and against all the defences you know at this point.

1. Begin in *porta di ferro mezana*.
2. You cut *fendente mandritto*.
3. Partner attempts to deflect your cut.
4. Deceive your partner's attempt to deflect your attack using one of the three combinations.

To begin with, perform this exercise without the defender sidestepping. When you have a comfortable command of the blade actions, allow your partner to sidestep on his deflection. This will change the possible angles for your main attack. Check that you are not pulling your feint (by cutting shorter than you should) by practising this exercise with full protective gear, and executing each cut to the touch (i.e. a gentle tap on the mask or other padded surface). On the occasions that your partner does not attempt a deflection you will see whether you were really threatening the target with your feint.

As a defender, you should treat every attack as a real attack, and defend yourself as above. If the successive or compound attack is properly done, there is no way you will be able to defend against it without either stepping away (generally a bad idea), or moving forwards into *giocco stretto*. If you are severely pressured, it is better to do successive deflections than to get hit, and this is quite common in freeplay. But strive to always answer his attack with your own.

Giocco Stretto Defences

As previously stated, *giocco stretto* or "close play," is the distance at which you can touch your opponent with your hand. This naturally includes all hand-strikes, pushes, locks, throws and breaks. The range of possible *giocco stretto* techniques is vast. For basic longsword practice, *giocco stretto* techniques have only one purpose: *to make it safe for you to hit your opponent with your sword*, usually with the hilt. In other words, why spend a fortune on a lovely shiny bit of steel if all you want to do is wrestle? At the beginner level, the techniques exist mainly to control your opponent's weapon long enough to enable you to hit him with impunity. The deflection that usually begins each defence should be done as you close in, with no particular emphasis on the blade contact: use it as a shield to advance under, rather than as a separate defence. Try to execute all the *giocco stretto* exercises in *mezzo tempo*; you should make body contact with him while he is still moving forwards.

Four Distances

As discussed in the Fencing Principles section, there are four specific *giocco stretto* distances. This exercise trains you to move into them at will, and incidentally is a great way to impress beginners, if done at speed. It can appear that the attacker, doing his level best, is being utterly humiliated by his opponent casually strolling by, invulnerable. Of course, any intelligent attacker will not launch an all-out cut at a stationary target, but try to create an opening line by forcing the defender to move. This is an exercise, not a fight-simulation, so the attacker must just keep to the one clear attack.

1. You are unarmed, and in the forward guard position with the left foot forwards. Your partner is armed, and in *posta di fenestra* with the left foot forwards.
2. Partner attacks with a *fendente mandritto* cut, passing forwards with the right foot as normal.
3. Pass diagonally forwards to the right, and place your left hand on your partners' sword wrist.
4. Repeat step 1 and 2, and on step 3, pass diagonally forwards to the right, and place your left elbow on your partners' right elbow, reaching over his left arm.
5. Repeat steps 1-2, and on step 3, pass circularly forwards so that your right shoulder is against his left. You may need to take a small step forwards with the left foot first.
6. Repeat steps 1 and 2, and on step 3, step forwards with your leading foot, and continue with a pass, so that you step behind your opponent, placing both hands on his shoulders.
7. Repeat steps 1-6 with the attacker starting with his right foot forwards, and passing with his left, cutting *fendente roverso*. Obviously, all stepping directions are effectively mirrored: i.e. step to the left each time.

Figures 8.24:
Four distance exercise versus Mandritto.
A- Wrist-distance.
B- Elbow-distance.

Figures 8.24:
C- Shoulder-distance.
D- Back-distance.

Figure 8.25:
Four distance exercise versus
a roverso *cut.*
A- Wrist-distance.
B- Elbow-distance.

Figures 8.25:
C- Shoulder-distance.
D- Back-distance.

So this exercise goes: wrist, elbow, shoulder, back; wrist, elbow, shoulder, back. Notice that as you are going forwards, the cut must miss you because you are no longer occupying the space at which the attack is directed. The timing is very important: you must arrive at your chosen distance *while his cut is still moving forwards*. This exercise will prepare you for the techniques described below.

The following *giocco stretto* exercises should be done from the same starting point as the deflection exercises: your partner establishes correct cutting distance, then attacks with *fendente mandritto*.

WRIST-DISTANCE

At beginner level, all wrist techniques are done against the sword-hand. This is because the weapon is mainly controlled by that hand as it is closer to the weapon's centre of gravity.

1. Begin in *porta di ferro mezana.*
2. Partner cuts *fendente mandritto.*
3. Execute a point-down deflection exactly as before, with a sidestep diagonally front-right into *fenestra* with the right foot.
4. At the moment of the deflection, reach forwards with your left hand under your right arm and grab his right wrist.
5. Step in with the left foot and execute a pommel strike to his face.
6. Repeat against *fendente roverso*: at step 4, on the deflection sidestep with the left foot, grab with the left hand, and at step 6, step in with the right foot and pommel to face.
7. Repeat against all cuts.

Figure 8.26: *A- Novati p. 161 / carta 22A, fig. 3.*

Figures 8.27:
Point-down deflection, wrist-distance pommel strike.

This is the most common continuation from the point-down deflection that resulted from yielding to the deflection. It should be practised as such, by continuing the yielding exercise with the pommel strike as detailed here.

1. Repeat as above, but at step 5, allow your sword to be pushed round, and cut, while controlling his sword hand with your left (see figs. 8.28 pp. 164-169).

2. Repeat as above with a point-up deflection to the inside, then to the outside. When deflecting on your inside line (i.e. your weapon is to your left, after deflecting either his *mandritto* with a point-up deflection to the inside, or his roverso with a point-up deflection to the outside), reach over your right arm with your left to grasp his sword hand, then continue with a belly cut followed by a pommel strike (see figs. 8.29 p. 167 and figs,. 8.31 p. 169).

When deflecting on your outside line, continue with either pommel strike, reverse *mulinello*, or direct cut (see figs. 8.30 p. 168)

Figure 8.28: *Point-down deflection, wrist distance cut.*

(Continued next page)

**Figures 8.28
(continued from
previous page):**
*Point-down deflection,
wrist distance cut.*

Figures 8.29:
Point-up deflection, inside line, wrist-distance, belly cut and pommel strike.

It is very important that you use your left hand just to control his sword: do not attempt any fancy locks or throws at this stage. You must be able to move comfortable into the correct distance at the correct time, keeping your centre closed while attacking his.

Figures 8.30:
Point-up deflection, inside line, wrist-distance, lever action direct cut.

Figures 8.31:
Point-up deflection, outside, wrist-distance, belly cut & pommel strike.

ELBOW DISTANCE

Beginner-level elbow-distance techniques are generally confined to a push against the outside of an extended arm, hyper-extending the joint, or enveloping one or both arms with your left. They are very sensitive to inaccuracies of distance: be very careful to apply the pressure exactly on the elbow joint.

Elbow Envelopment Lock:
1. Begin in *porta di ferro mezana*.
2. Partner cuts *fendente mandritto*.
3. Execute a point down deflection exactly as before, with a sidestep diagonally front-right into *fenestra* with the right foot.
4. At the moment of the deflection, step circularly forwards with your left foot while reaching forwards with your left arm and envelop both his arms at the level of his right elbow. Accurate positioning of your forearm against his elbow should allow you to easily fold his sword arm, effectively pinning both his arms and twisting him off balance.
5. Execute a pommel strike or draw-cut to his face.
6. Repeat against all *mandritto* cuts.

Figure 8.32: *Novati Fiore p. 163 / carta 22A, fig. 1.*

Figures 8.33:
Point-down deflection, inside line, elbow envelopment, finish with cut.

Elbow push

1. Repeat steps 1-3 of the previous exercise against *fendente roverso*.
2. At the moment of the deflection, sidestep slightly to the left with your right foot.
3. Step circularly forwards with your left foot, directing an open-handed push exactly on his right elbow (below & on p. 177).
4. As he is turning away, immediately cut fendente mandritto, with just your right hand on the sword.
5. Repeat against all cuts. Against *mandritti*, push against his left elbow.

Figures 8.34: *Fiore Novati p. 145 carta 14A, fig. 4.*

Figures 8.35:
Point-down deflection, outside line, elbow push, continue with cut.

Elbow envelopment throw

1. Repeat the first exercise, against *roversi* only.
2. At the moment of the deflection, circular step forwards with the left foot, and simultaneously envelop both his arms in your left arm.
3. Continue with a circular step with the right foot 180 degrees clockwise, pulling him off balance. Done at speed, with the proper hip rotation, this is a devastating throw. Be very careful.

Figure 8.36: *Detail of the reverse elbow envelopment shown in fig. D on p. 175.*

Figures 8.37: *Point down deflection, outside line, reverse elbow envelopment throw.*

You can also repeat as above with a lever-action deflection to the inside of the attack, then to the outside. When deflecting on your inside line (i.e. your weapon is to your left, after deflecting either his *mandritto* on the inside, or his *roverso* on the outside), reach *over* your right arm with your left to envelop his elbow, and continue a reverse *mulinello*, effecting a belly cut. When deflecting on your outside line, continue with the elbow push or the elbow envelopment throw.

Beginners tend to instinctively counter these techniques by not extending properly on their cut. If your partner is doing this, remind him gently that if he doesn't extend properly on the attack, he will not be able to do the proper counters to these techniques, nor would he be able to hit you in the first place. If he persists in pulling in his elbows, trap his right elbow against his body with your left hand instead of using the above techniques. He will eventually learn that it is a useless counter, and, hopefully, stop doing it.

Figures 8.38:
Point-up deflection, inside line, elbow distance.

Figures 8.39:
Point-up deflection, outside line, elbow-distance.

SHOULDER DISTANCE

There are many possible shoulder-distance techniques, though with a long-sword in hand, many of them become unnecessarily complex. We therefore will confine ourselves to one classic technique, known as the cross-buttock throw. This is exceedingly dangerous, as, if done properly, your partner will land on the back of his neck and promptly stop breathing. It is possible to learn to fall safely when thrown this way, but it is not an appropriate technique for teaching without direct contact with the student. So, in these exercises, enter properly, and take your partner's balance, but do not allow him to fall. The method below is the "friendly" throw: in a real fight you would of course rip his head backwards with your left hand, or smash your left forearm across his throat, at step 5.

1. Begin in *porta di ferro mezana*.
2. Partner cuts *fendente mandritto*.
3. Execute a point-up deflection to the outside exactly as before, with a sidestep diagonally forwards with the right foot.
4. Maintaining blade contact, circle his weapon down to the floor, while stepping in circularly with the left foot to position yourself behind him. It is vital that you step between his feet with your left foot, and jam your left shoulder against his right. Under no circumstances lose contact with his blade.
5. While stepping in, push your left arm forwards and up: your elbow should end in the middle of his chest. He is effectively scissored between your left elbow forcing his chest diagonally back and down, and your left leg preventing him from yielding (see fig.8.41b facing page).

Figures 8.40: *Fiore Novati p. 145 carta 14B, fig. 3.*

Figures 8.41:
Point-up deflection mandritto to shoulder distance, followed with a throw.

179

6. You can repeat the last drill against *fendente roverso*: at step 4, side-step right with the right foot on blade contact, then step in immediately with the left foot diagonally forwards to the left as you bear his sword down. Grip his sword-hand with your left, and execute the throw with a circular step anticlockwise with your right foot between his feet, while lifting your right elbow, or sword, into his chest (face in a non-friendly duel).

7. Repeat against all cuts against which you can get safely to the outside of the attack.

8. Repeat using *frontale* (see the exercise above **Getting to the outside with *Frontale*** p. 142-3, especially fig. 8.17d).

Figures 8.42: *Point-up deflection versus a* roverso, *step to shoulder distance, and throw.*

BACK-DISTANCE

Techniques done at back-distance are usually a chokehold or throat cut with the sword, or a neck throw. Frankly, they are not very useful in normal fencing conditions, but should eventually be learned as they were important in their time. The main uses of back-distance techniques are either to get immediately past your opponent and on to some other objective, to take down an opponent who is running at you, to take a hostage (particularly when faced by multiple attackers), or when your opponent is in armour, and you want to get him on the ground. In *Flos Duellatorum,* a back-distance technique is always preceded by an elbow-distance action, usually the push.

Figure 8.43: *Fiore Novati p. 162 carta 22B, fig. 3.*

COUNTERS

If you have really studied the above techniques, and taken the general principles to heart, a range of possible counters to each technique should be obvious. *Giocco stretto* techniques obey the same laws as blade techniques: you can avoid, deflect, or yield to an attack, provided you keep your balance correctly, your centre closed, and attack his centre. To illustrate this point, I will take you through a selection of counters (not an exhaustive list) to the elbow envelopment lock, done against your *fendente mandritto* attack. These are shown in order of their timing, from the earliest to the latest.

1. As his point-down deflection occurs, deceive it by pulling your hands back (shift into *posta breve*), and thrust under his sword (see fig. 8.44c p. 184).
2. As his deflection occurs, deceive it by changing the line of your cut to *mezano roverso* (see fig. 8.45 p. 185).
3. As his deflection occurs, step in to wrist-distance, and control his hands with your left, pushing them up and hitting him in the face with your pommel (see fig. p. 185).
4. After his deflection occurs, allow his left arm to reach over your arms; before he makes contact, pull back into *fenestra*, draw cutting along his ribs as you do so (see fig. 8.46 p. 185).
5. After his deflection occurs, allow his left arm to reach over your arms; as he makes contact, step through, pushing your hands towards the back of his head and turning them anticlockwise, creating an excellent lock, called the *chiave sottano*, or "under key" (see figs. 8.48 and 8.49p. 186).
6. After his deflection occurs, allow his left arm to reach over your arms; as he makes contact, allow the lock to occur, but free your left hand: palm-strike his jaw (use caution, this is a potential neckbreaker), and lift your left knee into his groin (carefully! this can end a friendship) (see fig. 8.50 p. 186).

Figures 8.44:
A- Guy attacks with fendente roverso,
Miika parries with a
point down deflection and...
B- ... closes to envelop Guy's arms.
The first counter to this is...
C- ...at the moment of the parry,
deceive it and thrust.

Figure 8.45:
Counter: deceive right-left.

Figure 8.46:
The Counter: wrist-push

Figure 8.47:
Counters: draw cut under arm.

Figure 8.48:
Counters: chiave sottano.

Figure 8.49:
Fiore Novati p. 164 / carta 23B, fig. 4.

Figure 8.50:
Counters: Jaw strike and knee to groin.

WORKING ON THE BLADE

Figure 8.51: *Engagement inside at* mezza spada.

ENGAGEMENT

The engagement is a fundamental fencing action that allows you to interpret your opponent's blade actions. However, it is not, as far as I am aware, documented in the historical treatises for this weapon. That said, against an opponent who offers his blade out for engagement, it is foolish to risk an all-out attack on the offered blade. He may slip your attack on his blade and strike. In this circumstance (probably more common now than it was then), it is safer and more practical to engage his blade, to feel him out. With the longsword, engagements are done either at half-sword (*mezza spada*), or three quarters down the blade (see fig. above).

Figure 8.52:
*Engagement at
three-quarters.*

Engagement can be made on the inside line, in which case his blade is to the left of yours, or on the outside line, in which case his blade will be to the right. In longsword fencing the most common occurrence of the engagement is when a fencer sticks on a deflection. In that case, the first person to continue usually wins. Remember, most longsword actions can be done from this position (the *incrosada*).

Engagement exercise
This is as much a distance exercise as a blade technique, though its main purpose is to teach you something of the nature of *sentimento di ferro*.

1. Begin with you both on guard in *posta longa*.
2. Engage the blades, in the third quarter, with your points threatening each other's faces.
3. Decide who has the initiative.
4. The attacker closes or widens the distance, threatening or creating a gap.
5. The defender maintains the same blade engagement, by adjusting the distance with his feet.
6. Repeat the exercise with the engagement at *mezza spada*.

The idea is to do it while maintaining a correct guard position, and by judging the feeling of contact on the blade. If you have a large, safe space, and fencing masks, this exercise can be done with your eyes closed.

When you have the hang of keeping the distance, work on the engagement itself. The engagement can be flat to flat, edge to edge (the attacker can try to get edge to flat), and can be changed by disengagements, cut-overs, or with pressure (see the next exercise for instructions).

ATTACKS ON THE BLADE
From the engagement, or at any time when your opponent is threatening you with his sword advanced (such as in *posta longa*) it is necessary to clear the way for your attack. In general, do not attack the blade unless you are already engaged, or your opponent is attacking with a thrust or cut: the blade is a very mobile target, and your opponent can easily deceive your attack if he is not commited to some other action. There are five blade actions you need to become familiar with at the basic level: pressure, disengagements, cutovers, beats, and hilt binds.

PRESSURE
Apply pressure to your opponent's blade to clear it out of your way, leaving your point on line.

DISENGAGEMENTS
The disengagement is done by slipping your point down, looping under his blade, and back up the other side to re-engage. This is not terribly common

Figure 8.53: *Pressure on the blade.*

with a longsword, as it leaves your hands unprotected for the instant that your sword is under his.

CUTOVERS

The cutover is done by slipping your point up and over his, re-engaging on the other side. This is the best way to change engagement with longswords. It may be easily converted into a beat (see below), or a cut down onto your opponent's forearm (see fig. next page).

BEATS

The beat is a short, sharp cut with your edge against his flat, to knock his blade aside for an instant. It must be hard enough to take his weapon off line to create the opportunity for your attack, but not so hard that if he deceives it (by disengaging underneath, avoiding the beat) you will leave yourself open.

HILT BINDS

Hilt binds are a way of using your crossguard to move his blade out of the way before you attack, and are often combined with grabbing his blade with your left hand. They may also be done from any crossing of the blades (*incrosada*), such as the moment of a deflection, and are usually done by shifting into *frontale* or *fenestra*.

Figures 8.54:
A cutover.

Figure 8.55:
Fiore Novati p. 157 / carta 20B, fig.2.

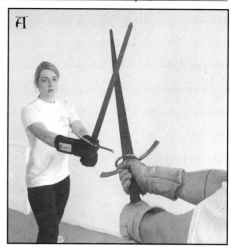

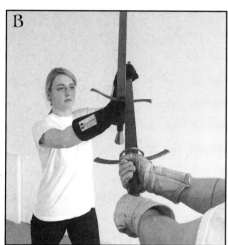

Figures 8.56: *Hilt collection.*

When "fencing on the blade" (i.e. with blades engaged), attacks on the blade normally precede any serious attack, because you have to clear his weapon out of the way. After you have mastered the pair exercises above as written, practise them from engagement. The distance will be different, which will affect the timing of your attacks and defences. Precede each attack with a beat, or a cutover followed by a beat.

WORKING OFF THE BLADE: USING THE GUARDS

"Fencing off the blade" was common in all early weapons styles that we know about, from the end of the thirteenth to the end of the sixteenth centuries (see for examples *Royal Armouries MS. I.33* from c. 1295, and dall'Agocchie's treatise of 1572). Essentially, the fencers begin out of distance, and circle around each other adopting various guards, until either an attack is launched, or they engage the blades. To fence off the blade effectively requires an intimate knowledge of the tactical opportunities afforded by all the guards taken by you and your opponent, and an exquisite judgement of distance. Practice all the pair exercises (except those beginning with an engagement) from all combinations of the guards you know. Find out for yourself what attacks and which defensive actions can be comfortably launched from each guard.

BREAKING THE GUARDS

This exercise is borrowed from the *Schola St. George* in California, and is a very safe and simple way of beginning to use the guards tactically.

1. Designate an "attacker" and a "defender."
2. Begin out of distance. Tha defender assumes any guard.
3. The attacker assumes a guard that he feels will force the defender to change his position (i.e. "break" his guard).
4. The attacker then assumes another guard that he feels will again break the defender's guard.

Of course, a wily "defender" can move into a guard that breaks the "attacker's" guard, reversing the roles. Play with this exercise, using no attacks at all. As you learn more guards (from the treatises or from the next book), incorporate them into the exercise.

Transitions between fencing off the blade to engagement can be done by offering your blade out for engagement in *posta longa* (make sure that you are in the necessary distance first), or by attacking. To get away from the engagement is risky: at the moment that you pull away, you are vulnerable, as you are creating an opening line. This can be used to your advantage in the following sample exercise:

USING THE GUARDS

1. Begin with both fencers in *posta longa*, left foot forwards, blades engaged.
2. Step back into *coda lunga e distesa*, keeping the left foot forwards.
3. At the same time as the opening is created, your partner should attack *fendente mandritto*.
4. At the same time as the *fendente mandritto* is launched, pass forwards circularly with the right foot, and also cut *fendente mandritto*, catching his *debole* on your *forte*, and hitting him on the mask (just as in the exercise "counterattack with the edge").

Chapter 9
Freeplay

We are lucky to live in an age where, in theory at least, might does not equal right. In most cultures, the duelling code has fallen into disuse and we are not expected to defend our honour with a sword. In addition, the weapons of self-defence have changed out of all recognition, so it is safe to assume that none of us will ever use a longsword in earnest. But to fully understand its use in history, and to test our own level of skill, it is vital that swordsmen in training have the opportunity for freeplay. It bears repeating that the purpose of every fencing match you undertake, unless it is a frank and earnest encounter with sharps, is to improve your swordsmanship, not to win.

The trap that most beginners fall into, as I did myself, is the realisation early on that practising technique while fencing, rather than relying on your wits and instinct, can often mean losing a match you could win. These lost bouts can be an embarrassment, and can certainly lead you to doubt the validity of so-called "good technique." This is why I believe it is a bad idea for relatively untrained students to freeplay too often in uncontrolled conditions. Not all instructors will agree with me here, because their emphasis on teaching swordplay as the art of self-defence leads them to treat all bouts as practice for the real thing: if losing equals dying, the student must be trained to win at all costs, from the outset. I disagree with this approach because it is predicated on two mistaken surmises: that freeplay is only fight-simulation, and that the will to win is the main component in winning.

If we go back a couple of hundred years to the fencing schools of the eighteenth century, we find a totally different attitude towards freeplay. These masters were teaching the art of survival in a culture where everyone went armed, and every gentleman was expected to be ready to defend his honour with his life. Yet in those salles it was the height of bad manners to brutalise or wound an opponent.[1] During freeplay, one might even be expected to delay a riposte to allow your opponent to return to guard. This was in part a safety consideration in an age when fencing masks were uncommon. But it was also because the instructors at these schools clearly believed that the purpose of freeplay was to practise good technique, not to score touches. There has never been a good excuse for unsafe play. The first schools of fence to emphasise winning in the salle, that I know of, were mid-twentieth-century sport-fencing schools. An interesting coincidence: only fencers who were never likely to fight to the death were trained to fight only to win in practice. The fifteenth-century masters do not cover this point specifically, though in the introduction to *Flos Duellatorum*, Fiore states "in techniques that are only for practice, the holds are "holds of love," and not "holds of anger."[2]

Instincts make a fighter, but trained responses make a swordsman. Every manual on survival I have ever read, be it on first aid, survival in extreme conditions, or combat, recognise as their first rule, *stop and think!* If the situation panics you, or you just rush off according to instinct, you may well make the situation worse. Concentrating on technique, even when it means receiving more hits than you give in freeplay, will, in time, help you achieve your full potential as a swordsman, and stop you from getting stuck in the rut of instinctive fighting.

Once you are able to fight without reliance on instinct, maintaining physical and mental equilibrium throughout, it becomes possible to be trained in tactics and strategy. This includes the development of insight, cunning and downright deviousness. As when learning to drive, before you can make the best and clearest decision about what to do you must practice control of the vehicle until your will can be implemented automatically. This gives you the mental equilibrium not to panic when a juggernaut fills your rear-view mirror; so too with swordplay.

Of course, whenever you face off with someone, you are trying to hit and not be hit. But an essential prerequisite to the understanding of swordsmanship is the knowledge tantamount to faith that the best way to overcome real opponents is to get all the physical and mental technical practice you can while your life is not at stake. Then you will be able to apply your cunning when it really matters.

TACTICS: HOW TO FENCE

There are two contrasting styles of fencing: the creative, in which you allow your opponent to fence at his best, bringing him out so you can hit him; and the destructive, where you seek to completely annihilate his offensive and defensive capability as quickly as possible. Each has merit: the former is the artist's approach, the latter the fighter's.[3] A good swordsman should be able to use both.

The creative approach requires the utmost detachment and skill; it requires you to subtly induce your opponent to attack. This can be done in two ways:

Engagement: offer an engagement; when the blades make contact, allow him to initiate attacks on the blade. Wait for him to commit himself before you counter.

Provocation: this includes offering openings for him to attack (onto your prepared defence, naturally), or attacking him. If the latter, be careful not to press too hard: you may force a wild and unexpected response. Apply just sufficient pressure to force him to act.

The creative approach does not imply using weak technique; on the contrary. Your technique must be absolutely as vigorous, as well applied, and as solidly grounded as when using the destructive approach. In the Salle, I insist on the creative approach because it offers the greatest challenge to the swordsman, and allows the finest technical actions. An example that springs to mind is a formal duel I engaged in with Mr. Jared Kirby for full membership of the *Dawn Duellists Society* on January 29th 2001, with Mr. Gareth Hunt and Maestro Paul Macdonald as seconds. We were both fencing at our best. One sequence, at full speed and with intent to win, went like this: I attacked, to draw his counter; as he countered, I closed, enveloping his sword with my left arm, and aimed a pommel-strike at his mask; the moment his sword was no longer useful to him, he let go with both hands, and disarmed me, immediately using my weapon against me; I went past, taking enough distance to give me time for a proper grip on his sword, and we continued fencing with each other's weapons, without pause, until the next touch was scored. In all, the action took a couple of seconds, but in that time there were three blade actions, two disarms and one pommel strike, all in the heat of the moment. That was truly longsword fencing.

The destructive approach is the best way to win fights quickly against most fencers, though against a swordsman well-trained in the creative approach it is unlikely to be successful.

Engagement: offer an engagement; when the blades make contact, gain control of his sword with a hilt bind, a beat, or opposition, closing in until you force him off balance.

Provocation: this includes offering openings for him to attack (onto your prepared defence, naturally), or attacking him, forcing him to either deflect, in which case you should ideally deceive his defence and hit him, or counterattack, in which case close the line and keep moving forwards and hit him.

You may have noticed a common thread in the destructive approach: close in and hit him! In general, I prefer to fence creatively. Occasionally, when it is necessary to make a point, or when it is my only hope against a superior opponent in a duel that matters (which is very rare), I will use the destructive approach. Some fencers, trained only to deal with creative fencing, cannot withstand a domineering opponent.

Whenever possible, try to stick to creative fencing: it will give you the best experience, and the most memorable bouts. Remember that every action has many counters, and that the object of your freeplay is to learn swordsmanship: your overall strategic goal is to improve as a swordsman.

The basic tactical rule when fencing is:
1. Do not get hit.
2. Hit, but only when necessary to obey the first rule.

At *giocco largo* this is achieved by:
1. Counterattack: against an attack, counterattack.
2. Deflect: against an attack or counterattack, deflect.
3. Deceive or Yield: against a deflection, deceive or yield.
4. Opening line: only attack an opening line, or to create an opening line.
5. Avoid: avoid when possible, stepping away from blade contact.

And at *giocco stretto* by:
1. Attack the centre.
2. Use all parts of the weapon offensively.
3. Use hands and feet to strike, and the left arm to grapple or envelop.
4. Do not wrestle: use unarmed techniques to incapacitate him just long enough to hit him somewhere vital with something hard.

OPPONENTS: WHO TO FENCE

It is necessary to choose your opponents with care. There is nothing to be gained from fencing with someone whose ego depends on beating you; unless you are much more skilful than them, their sheer viciousness may drag you down to their level. A little earnest competitive edge does no harm on occasion, but the moment your opponent refuses to acknowledge hits, or attempts inappropriately dangerous technique, stop. You have nothing to learn from them. Do not be afraid to walk away from a bout.

I group opponents into six categories that you should learn to recognise, and embrace or avoid as necessary.

1. The good opponent with less skill than you. This type has the right mental approach, and his ego well under control. Inexperience makes him unpredictable, perhaps even dangerous. Make sure sufficient protection is worn, and do not humiliate him by demolishing him. Use his unpredictability to train your responses to the unforeseen, while giving him the chance to try out what he knows. As the result of the match is not in question, what matters is how it progresses. Do not get complacent.

2. The bad opponent with less skill than you. This one has taken up the longsword because he wants to fight with an impressively dangerous weapon. If your skill is sufficient to run rings around him, take him on. He may learn from your detachment, and in

time come to a more mature understanding of the advantages of technique. If you are not that good yet, avoid fencing with him because every "victory" over "technique" will subconsciously reinforce his attitude that fighting instincts are all he needs.

3. The good opponent with about your level of skill. Bouts with this type can go on for ever, but are always rewarding. Enjoy pitting your skill and cunning against his. One smallsword duel I fenced with Mr. Gareth Hunt, an instructor at the DDS, went on for 80 minutes, in which time a total of eight hits were scored (5-3). We were just being careful. Everybody except us was bored by the end, but we loved it.

4. The bad opponent with about your level of skill. Watch out: this is where most injuries occur. Because you are evenly matched in skill and this opponent is desperate to win, he will try almost anything to make a hit. I have known such opponents literally leap at my neck with their hands, trying to throw me full tilt onto a concrete floor, during a supposedly friendly unarmed sparring session. The nice ones are invariably terribly embarrassed and apologetic after injuring you, and honestly have no idea they are being stupid and dangerous. The need to win just eclipses rational thought or is even disguised as rational thought, so they genuinely do not understand what might be wrong with their attitude.

5. The good, more skilful opponent. A joy to fence, partly because no-one can reasonably expect you to win. With the pressure off, you can learn a huge amount about the application of technique, and particularly strategy. The match will not be over as quickly as possible, because this opponent is busy practising technique on you.

6. The bad, more skilful opponent. Otherwise known as a bully. Fencing these people is usually a waste of time, as neither of you learn anything. Fortunately it is normally over very quickly, as they just pile in and win immediately, to prove to themselves that they can defeat someone with less skill and experience than them. Avoid this type if you can. Fortunately, their development is arrested by their attitude, so it is usually possible to surpass them in time, relegating them to type 2.

RULES OF ENGAGEMENT

Once you have agreed to fence with someone, it is important to agree on rules of engagement. This is partly to ensure safety, and partly to create an environment in which you can learn. The two most simple rules are these: confine your moves to the safety limits of your protective gear and to the technical range of the least trained combatant. In other words, do not allow face-thrusts when wearing open helms, or throws when one of you is not trained to fall safely. The rules can be adapted further to develop specific aspects of technique: for instance, you may not allow any close quarters work at all, or even restrict allowable hits to one small target. The idea is to come to a clear, common-sense agreement before facing off. You are only ready for no-holds-barred, totally "authentic" fight simulation, when you can enter such a fight with your judgement unimpaired. Following the rules of engagement will not make you soft, nor will it dull your edge if it comes to the real thing; rather it will develop self-control.

These rules apply to all fencing:
1. Agree on a mutually acceptable level of safety.
2. Wear at least the minimum amount of safety gear commensurate with rule 1.
3. Confine allowable technique to those within the limits of your equipment.
4. Confine allowable technique to the technical ability of the least trained combatant.
5. Appoint either an experienced student or one of the combatants to preside over the bout.
6. Agree on allowable targets.
7. Agree on what constitutes a "hit."
8. Agree on priority in the event of simultaneous hits. Usually it is better to allow a fatal blow before a minor wound, but simultaneous hits should be avoided whenever possible.
9. Agree on the duration of the bout either in terms of hits, such as first to five, or in real time.
10. Acknowledge all hits against yourself. This can be done by raising the left arm, or by stopping the bout with a salute, or by calling "Halt!" and telling your opponent where and how you think he hit you.
11. Maintain self-command at all times.

COMBAT SITUATIONS

With the longsword, there are four types of combat situation: the unarmoured duel, the armoured duel, battle, and street defence (I do not count the tournament because it is not combat but competition, and is designed to simulate one of the two types of duel). To fully appreciate the wonderful diversity of this weapon, one should train at all four, though I feel that the highest expression of the art is found in the unarmoured duel.

The unarmoured duel is an arranged fight with two combatants, neither wearing any protective gear. The whole body is obviously open to attack, though some target areas are more lethal than others. When simulating an unarmoured duel, it is vital to remember that the protection you are wearing does not exist when deciding hits, yet you must confine your attacks and the allowable hits to protected areas. I normally recommend that simultaneous hits are both awarded (unless only one is "fatal", in which case only that one is awarded). This encourages a more defensive, survival-oriented style. This style has relatively little to do with military actions, and there is no way to know how common such engagements were in the longsword period. However, Fiore, Vadi, and the German treatises that I have seen include extensive unarmoured sections and techniques that are totally inappropriate for a crowded, battle-type situation.

The armoured duel derives mainly from judicial combat, though many of its skills come from the battlefield. It requires a sufficiently different use of the longsword that Vadi recommends an adapted longsword type called the *spada en arme*. This is a weapon designed mainly for half-sword technique, with the last four inches of blade expanding into a sharpened leaf shape, and with spiked crossguard and pommel. The idea is largely to close in and position your attack carefully into the chinks of your opponent's armour. The other major historical approach is to use a bludgeoning weapon such as a mace or war hammer to batter your opponent through his armour. Of course, a good sword blow, or at least much of its energy, can go through a helmet or other armour.[4] Armour is a weapon in its own right, and you will learn to ignore hits that cannot hurt you if it allows you to make an attack that will go through. When freeplaying with the longsword in armour, the difficulty lies in judging what constitutes a hit. If the reason you are fencing in harness is to practice documented armoured technique, then only hits to unprotected areas should count. There is really no point in putting on lots of heavy, expensive plate or mail if a cut across the breastplate counts.[5] I would therefore only practice armoured technique with very competent, calm opponents, and play to touches on the vulnerable spots. Much armoured work is done at very close quarters, so you can precisely position your thrust. Throws and grapples are also very common and exceptionally dangerous. I therefore urge you to be very, very careful whom you practise with, and if possible wear padded protection over those vulnerable spots (historically these would have been defended by mail gussets). A good way to kill a man in harness is to throw him and then slip your dagger through his visor: historically accurate technique, but impossible to practice safely.

Those of you who have worn full plate armour will know that it is not that heavy, and, contrary to popular belief, a fully armoured man can run, jump, roll, even dance techno (I have seen this with my own eyes). As a result, armoured duelling is fast, hard and dangerous. When practised in the Middle Ages, it was a very popular spectator sport, and even in friendly jousts knights would occasionally be killed.

Battle is practically impossible to simulate realistically. The closest we can get is re-enactment, which affords a splendid opportunity to practise against an enormous variety of training and fighting styles. It is, however, invariably inaccurate in that rules allow hits that a fully armoured man would scarcely notice, and, for valid safety reasons, most of the techniques taught by Fiore and Vadi are forbidden. For instance, many re-enactment societies that allow steel weapons do not permit grappling, head hits or thrusts, and it is considered poor form to go for the chinks not the armour. I therefore use battles as opportunities to practise unarmoured street defence and mêlée work. Though there is no way to accurately simulate genuine battle conditions safely, it is possible to work out group strategies, and to practise the teamwork element of battle training. Re-enactments are also a good way to discover that training pays off: most re-enactors do not train in correct swordplay technique, and are therefore usually flummoxed when confronted by it. I have often seen relative beginners trained in correct technique take on experienced re-enactors, and defeat them in seconds. It is important to keep in mind that many re-enactors are essentially actors putting on a display, and their meticulous safety limitations restrict their training considerably.

Street defence is the one type of fighting where surprise may be truly present. No-one in the line of battle is truly surprised by the enemy, unless they are in some way ambushed (in which case the techniques of street defence combined with knowledge of armoured work is the only preparation). In its time, the longsword may have been called upon to defend the life of its owner in the streets and alleys of European cities. Before the development of the *spada da lato*, and subsequently the rapier, the longsword was probably carried in times of peace as well as war, to deal with assassins and footpads. This style of combat is relatively difficult to simulate, but is perfectly possible to practice in theory. *Flos Duellatorum*, for example, includes ways of using your sword defensively against an attacker with a dagger, while your weapon is still in its scabbard! The rules of unarmoured and armoured work may apply depending on your assailant's choices of garb. Essentially, you must attack and disable as many opponents as you can, as quickly as possible, and using whatever advantages of terrain you can muster. The fact is that however good you are, a properly orchestrated attack by just three people is almost impossible to defend against: while your sword is hitting one of them, it cannot be hitting the others, who are able to hit you. The surest way to defend yourself is to prevent the attack from being properly orchestrated, either by taking the initiative, choosing the terrain so that only one may attack at a time, or by trickery. There are many instances in history of gangs being beaten off by a lone swordsman, but, invariably, the attack was not properly orchestrated and the defender would usually receive his share of wounds.[6]

Courtesy

One of the hallmarks of a good swordsman is courtesy. It does not matter what you think of your opponent (though it is usually safer to overestimate their skill) but it is essential to your development as a swordsman that you cultivate a respect for the weapon and its use. All bouts, however informal, should begin with the salute. After the bout you should always shake hands. I often acknowledge particularly good hits against me with a quick salute, rather than just raising my arm.

Afterword

The moment an opinion on any subject is written down, it is vulnerable. Language is paradoxically nebulous yet precise: I know what I mean, and you may understand what I mean, but there is no way to be certain that the most detailed and precise observations, remarks, or instructions will not be transformed by the context of the reader into something quite other than my intention. I have no doubt that much of what I say here will cause the average reader to nod their head and mutter internally "hmm, that seems reasonable." I am equally sure that there will be many points where some readers will disagree, violently or otherwise, and some will even take offence.

This book contains enough basic theory, background, and technical instruction to get any reasonably intelligent, committed and able-bodied reader off to a good start in the study of western swordsmanship. That said, my understanding and formulation of fencing theory, the precise way I execute basic techniques, and my didactic method have changed immeasurably in the last ten years, and there is no reason to suppose that that process of improvement has stopped (I hope). I have also been compelled to leave out a vast range of techniques, and many of the more subtle theoretical points. This book is just a beginning, intended for the complete novice. It is also a snapshot of a work in progress, and I ask the indulgence of my readers to focus on the sound basics and solid practicality of the techniques within, and to overlook and forgive the many human errors that this book must contain.

Part of the reason for writing this book, other than to counter some of the truly horrible misinterpretations of my beloved art that are already out there, is to expose my method and myself to the informed and invaluable scrutiny, criticism and evaluation of my peers in this field. We suffer in this art from a lack of experienced, trained instructors: they do exist, but in small numbers scattered across the globe. So just as it is very hard for a beginner to find out the right path to correct historical fencing, it is still harder for the few professionals in this field to get the stimulation and supervision we need. I ask all those that consider themselves to be experts in this field to freely challenge any assertion I make in this book, so that my book, my students and I may benefit from their experience.

Appendix A
In a Nutshell

In the Salle

1. Safety: safety first! Never hit anyone by accident or in anger.
2. Respect: for your opponents, your training partners, and the weapon. This is demonstrated by courtesy.

When fencing

1. Do not get hit.
2. Hit, but only when necessary to obey the first rule.

Fundamentals

1. Guard: Never sacrifice your guard position. Keep your back straight and your legs bent, mantaining your balance and ability to fight at all times. Remember Fiore's *Elephant*.
2. Centre: Close your centre, attack his centre. This is done by always retaining opposition: keep the *forteza* between his sword and you: keep the *debole* towards your opponent's centre.
3. Oppose or Yield: only oppose strength to weakness; yield to strength.

Giocco largo with a longsword

1. Counterattack: against an attack, counterattack.
2. Deflect: against an attack or counterattack, deflect.
3. Deceive or Yield: against a deflection, deceive or yield.
4. Opening line: only attack an opening line, or to create an opening line.
5. Avoid: avoid when possible, stepping away from blade contact.

Giocco stretto with a longsword

1. Attack the centre.
2. Use all parts of the weapon offensively.
3. Use hands and feet to strike, and the left arm to grapple or envelop.
4. Do not wrestle: use unarmed techniques to incapacitate him just long enough to hit him somewhere vital with something hard.

Troubleshooting

If a technique is not working, the problem always lies in one or more of the following areas:

1. Distance.
2. Timing.
3. Configuration.
4. Direction.

The Basic SESH warm-up

Joint loosening

1. **Knee rotations**: begin in forward stance. Place both hands on your front knee. By pushing your weight gently back and forth between the feet, turn the knee gently 15 times in a horizontal circle clockwise then anticlockwise. Repeat on other side.

2. **Swinging**: Feet wide apart, weight on one bent leg, arms totally relaxed, push across from one leg to the other, bending the knee and turning your hips and shoulders. The arms swing naturally. Keep your back straight, head up, and let the motion of your arms be driven only by your legs. You will feel your back twisting gently, stretching the muscles around your spine (GENTLY!).

3. **Neck rotations**: turn your head clockwise six times, then the other way. Do not tip the head back. Make the circles just large enough to feel a slight stretch in the muscles.

4. **Neck turns**: Look over your right shoulder, then your left, in turn. Six times each side.

5. **Neck tips**: look up at the sky, then down at the floor, stretching in turn your throat and your neck.

6. **Neck tilts**: tilt your head to one side as if to lay your ear on your shoulder. Keep the shoulders down.

7. **Arm rotations**: keeping the arms relaxed and straight (but do not lock the elbows), swing them from the shoulders 12 times around backwards, then twelve times forward, then 12 times right arm forward, left arm backwards, then reverse.

8. **Open chest**: cross your arms loosely over your chest, then swing them horizontally backwards, then back across, 12 times. Alternate so that the right hand crosses above then below the left.

9. **Hip rotations**: hands on hips, feet shoulder width. Rotate the hips 20 times anticlockwise, then reverse. This should be done with bent knees, but the lower back should be doing practically all the work.

10. **Back rotations**: widen your stance, reach up to the sky with both hands, then, keeping the legs slightly bent, but not flexing them, rotate the whole body 9 times each way, describing as large a circle as possible with your hands. The centre of rotation is the hips and lower back. Change direction when the hands are by the floor, and finish in that position.

Warming the body

11. **Scoops**: with your feet wide apart, place your hands on the floor shoulder-width apart and walk them forwards, leaving your feet where they are. You should now be in a press-up position,

but with your legs spread and your hips in the air. Rock your weight back onto your feet, leaving your hands where they are. From here, breathing in, scoop down towards the floor, bending the arms, then rise up to a cobra position, with your head up, back bent backwards, hips near the floor, arms and legs straight,. Breathing out, reverse the motion so the weight returns to the feet and your hips rise up. Beginners may find doing just one of these very difficult. Aim to build up your strength over many months, eventually you should be able to do at least 20.

12. **Ski-running**: stand left foot and right arm forward, left arm and right foot back. Keeping your feet parallel, and swinging your arms back and forth in time to your feet, "ski" on the spot with as much length and smoothness as possible. 25 repetitions should get the blood moving.

13. **Star jumps**: standing with feet together and hands by your sides, swiftly touch your hands together above your head and open your legs wide. Immediately return to the start position. Repeat 25 times.

You should now be reasonably warmed-up, with the major joints active and supple. If you feel any particularly stiff bits, loosen those up before stretching.

Stretches

14. **Feet together**, reach up as high as you can, then keeping the legs straight, bend down as far as is comfortable. You will feel this stretch in the backs of your legs or in your spine. It doesn't matter: the stiffest part will be getting stretched. Hold for 20 seconds, then slowly return to upright.

15. **Repeat the above exercise, but first cross one leg over the other**, feet together and pointing forwards. This focuses the stretch in the back of the rear leg. Hold for 20 seconds, then rise up and change the feet over, and repeat.

16. **Inside stretch**: open the legs, keeping the feet parallel, as far as is comfortable, then sink down onto one foot, keeping both feet flat on the ground, and your extended leg straight. This stretches the inside of the extended leg. Hold for 20 seconds, then change sides.

17. **Lunge stretch**: with your legs still spread, turn one foot out so that it is at right angles to the other. Bend the knee, sinking almost all of your weight to one foot. Keep your back straight, and the rear leg extended. Both feet are flat on the floor, and the bent front knee remains directly above the ankle. Hold for 20 seconds, then change sides.

18. **Toe-up**: feet parallel and wide apart, shift the weight to one foot, sinking as low as possible. Allow the unweighted foot to turn up, toes pointing to the ceiling. If this does not stretch you, lean down and reach with your hands for the upright foot. Hold for 20 sec-

onds, then change sides. Keep the heel of the supporting foot on the ground. It doesn't matter if you can't go very low. Keep your hands off the floor. This is also a balance exercise.

19. **Heel-up**: return to the lunge position, but allow the back heel to rise, dropping and flexing the rear knee. You should feel this in the front of the rear thigh. Hold for 20 seconds, then change sides.

20. Return to a wide standing position, and repeat the swinging exercise.

This warm-up should leave you feeling warm, loose, and relaxed. It takes about 12-15 minutes, when you get the hang of it. This is not intended as strength or aerobic training, though it will improve your general condition (assuming you're not already very fit). Remember to breathe deeply and easily throughout the warm-up, and be gentle with the stretches. It is also important to move smoothly from one position to the next.

After doing your footwork practice, it is a good idea to warm up your shoulders, elbows and wrists before taking up the sword. Repeat steps 2-8 as above, then stretch the shoulders and arms:

1. **Shoulder stretch**: reach up behind your back with your left hand, reach over your right shoulder with your right hand, and link hands between your shoulder-blades. If you can't manage this straight away, use a stick, a towel or something similar to connect your hands. Hold for 20 seconds, then change sides.

2. Extend your left hand in front of you, palm up, thumb pointed to the left. Place your right hand underneath it, also palm up, and grasp your left thumb with your right fingers. Use your right hand to twist your left arm anticlockwise, keeping the elbow straight. Hold for 20 seconds, then change sides.

3. Extend your left hand in front of you, palm down, thumb pointed to the right. Place your right hand on top, and hook your right thumb over the little-finger edge of your left hand. Use your right hand to twist your left arm clockwise, keeping the elbow straight. Hold for 20 seconds, then change sides.

4. Shake out your arms, clench and unclench your fists a few times, checking for sore spots.

The warm-up exercises and stretches are not specific to Western swordsmanship, neither are they an exhaustive list. Feel free to import any warm-up exercises from other martial arts or sports that you have found work for you. Every body is different; try to find the combination of exercises and stretches that suits yours the best.

Appendix C
Training Schedule

Constructing a Training Schedule

The structure of your ideal training schedule will change as you become more proficient, but to get the most out of this book, I would advise that you practise along these lines.

Firstly, establish regular training times. Ideally this should be two hours a day, but in the real world, with non-professional swordsmen, it is more likely to be once or twice a week. Once you have established your schedule, stick to it. In general, little and often is better for re-programming muscle memory than an occasional 8-hour mega-session.

The method in this book is laid out in the order that you should practice: warm-up, body-mechanics, footwork, solo sword practice, pair exercise, free-play. Do not expect to cover everything in one session, and do not try to do every exercise of each type each time. Progress gradually through the exercises in the order that they are written.

The first set of 8 sessions should look like this:
Warm-up: 10-15 minutes.
Body-mechanics exercises: 20-30 minutes.
Footwork exercises: 20-30 minutes.
Solo sword practice: 20-30 minutes.
Finish with a warm-down emphasising stretches.

Then, depending on how well you have mastered the basic solo practice, the second set of 8 sessions should go like this:
Warm-up: 10-15 minutes.
Body-mechanics exercises: 15-20 minutes.
Footwork exercises: 15-20 minutes.
Solo sword practice: 20-30 minutes.
Pair exercises: 20-30 minutes.
Finish with a warm-down emphasising stretches.

Increase the amount of time spent on pair exercises in the third set of 8 sessions:
Warm-up: 10-15 minutes.
Body-mechanics exercises: 10-15 minutes.
Footwork exercises: 10-15 minutes.
Solo sword practice: 10-15 minutes.
Pair exercises: 30-40 minutes.
Finish with a warm-down emphasising stretches.

When you are comfortable with all the pair exercises and beginning to work out the counters, introduce light freeplay into about one training session in four. To counterbalance the detrimental effect that faster, more random practice such as freeplay has on your basic, core technique, reintroduce more basic solo training to your schedule, both immediately after freeplay, and in subsequent sessions, so in any four sessions you will have one including freeplay, one from the second set, and two from the third. So the fourth set of 8 sessions will go something like this:

First session:
    Warm-up: 10-15 minutes.
    Body-mechanics exercises: 10-15 minutes.
    Footwork exercises: 10-15 minutes.
    Solo sword practice: 10-15 minutes.
    Pair exercises: 20-30 minutes.
    Freeplay: 10 minutes.
    Slow pair exercises: 10 minutes.
    Finish with a warm-down emphasising stretches.

Second session:
    Warm-up: 10-15 minutes.
    Body-mechanics exercises: 15-20 minutes.
    Footwork exercises: 15-20 minutes.
    Solo sword practice: 20-30 minutes.
    Pair exercises: 20-30 minutes.
    Finish with a warm-down emphasising stretches.

Third session:
    Warm-up: 10-15 minutes.
    Body-mechanics exercises: 10-15 minutes.
    Footwork exercises: 10-15 minutes.
    Solo sword practice: 10-15 minutes.
    Pair exercises: 30-40 minutes.
    Finish with a warm-down emphasising stretches.

Fourth session:
    Warm-up: 10-15 minutes.
    Body-mechanics exercises: 10-15 minutes.
    Footwork exercises: 10-15 minutes.
    Solo sword practice: 10-15 minutes.
    Pair exercises: 30-40 minutes.
    Finish with a warm-down emphasising stretches.

Repeat the pattern to make eight sessions.

Then replace the third session with another like the first, so that in the next set of eight sessions there will be four including freeplay, two where you go back to basics, and two where you focus on pair drills.

The above schedule covers 40 two-hour sessions. Once you have practised that much you should have a fair idea where your weaknesses are, and you will find that the solution to those weaknesses will be found in one or other of the basic drills. So adjust your schedule to fit your own needs (and those of your training partner or group), to work on the aspects of swordsmanship you find most difficult. You may find it useful to keep a record of when and what you have practised. Remember that every session should include a warm-up, basic footwork exercises, basic solo sword-handling exercises, and a warm-down.

NOTES

CHAPTER 1

[1] This may seem a little harsh, but I witnessed the 2001 World Championship finals in men's foil and women's sabre: it looked absolutely awful, and the most sophisticated action in either bout was a parry riposte. There was no sense of the weapons being treated as if they were sharp, and precious little skill being shown: the bouts came down to speed, anger, and luck. My coaches would have been disgusted with me if I ever fenced like that.

[2] The printing conventions of this period include the use of various signs above one letter to denote another missing letter. Here, "õ" clearly represents "on". This convention remains to this day in the use of the apostrophe, and was more widespread in the past. In the later sections dealing with the handwritten Italian sources, the use of various squiggles is more common, and I have attempted to render these using the fonts available to better represent the original texts.

[3] George Silver, *Paradoxes of Defence* (1599), p. 2.

[4] This approach is called often called experimental archaeology: basically, students adopt the armour and weapons of the historical combatants and then fight with one another to see what is possible. Although these groups have created some interesting martial arts based on historical equipment, the techniques practiced are largely optimized for very different rules frameworks. This method has undoubted virtues, and should be included in the research of all Western martial artists seeking to recreate lost styles, but if unsupported by research its application in a historical context is open to question.

[5] As far as I know the earliest example of this kind of thing may be found in *Life* magazine from 1948; in a story entitled "Two Bored Britons Battle in Armor" you can see Adrian Conan Doyle (Sir Arthur's son), and Douglas Ash, wearing original sixteenth-century plate harness and bashing each other with what are probably original seventeenth-century swords (though they apparently did not attempt to recreate historical fencing methods).

[6] I remember one rapier bout with a German gentleman visiting the Dawn Duellists Society in Edinburgh. I fenced under the accepted convention that we were using blunt weapons for safety, but scoring touches *as if they were sharp*. So I was very surprised when he ignored **five** consecutive thrusts to the centre of his chest, closed in, and managed to put me in a wrestling hold, with my right arm pinned between his legs. I had transferred my sword to my left hand, and was literally beating him over the mask with it, yelling "you are dead you idiot!" (those may not have been my *exact* words) over and over again before it was established that we had different ideas about what constituted a fencing match.

[7] *Salle* is abbreviated from the French *salle d'armes*, literally "room of weapons", and is generally used in fencing circles to denote the training hall.

[8] "The School of European Swordsmanship, Helsinki" (acronym SESH) is my registered trade-name (toiminimi).

[9] Freeplay, free fencing, and free assault all refer to what other martial arts call sparring: safe (within reason), controlled, but unrehearsed mock-fighting.

[10] It is necessary to establish a consistent nomenclature for fencing terms. Wherever practicable, I use the historical terminology of the weapon in question. Most technical names, such as guard positions, cutting angles, etc., are taken from the core treatises for the weapon in question. The idea is to retain the feel of the style, and to promote awareness of the historical sources. Some groups have established a common set of terms for all weapons: this is another valid approach. I prefer to teach using weapon-specific terminology. So a cut may be *fendente mandritto* with a longsword, and the same cut be called *squalembro mandritto* when using a rapier.

[11] See J. Chrisoph Amberger's *The Secret History of the Sword* (1999), especially pp. 113-119.

[12] "Spiritualists" normally refers to people who practice spiritualism, a nineteenth-century cult

that conducted seances to contact the dead. However, it is too suggestive and useful a term to be condemned forever to such limited use so I am here reclaiming it to describe people who are concerned with spiritual matters.

[13] This modern perspective contrasts with the medieval knight Geoffrey de Charny, who in his *Demands Pour la Joute, Le Tournois et La Guerre* divided fighting into three types: jousts, tourneys, and war. This is probably closer to the general perception in the fifteenth-century, but is less useful when considering unarmoured combat, which is the main focus of this book.

[14] There are many references to the "laws of war" which also governed duels, though it is believed that these laws were not written down before Honoret Bonet codified some of them during the latter 14th century in his Tree of Battles. Geoffrey de Charny refers over and over again to the "Law of Arms", though he polled contemporary knights for their opinion as to what the law was on each particular point. See especially Steven Muhlberger, *Jousts & Tournaments: Charny and Chivalric Sport in 14th century France* (Mar. 2003 Chivalry Bookshelf). See also Amberger p. 116, and Baron César de Bazancourt's *Secrets of the Sword* (1998) pp. 163-166 (regarding the admissibility of left-hand parries in epée duelling).

[15] Ewart Oakeshott, *Records of the Medieval Sword*, (1991) p. 1.

[16] Conferring knighthood with the sword is a post-medieval device: in variations on the medieval ceremony, knighthood is thought to have been conferred by the girding of the military belt (*adoubement*, hence "dubbing"), or by the affixing of spurs (hence the phrase, "to win one's spurs"). Brian R. Price, personal correspondence.

[17] See especially the writings of Raymond Lull, the 14th century knight-come-cleric who penned the far-reaching and influential *Book of Knighthood and Chivalry*. See also the anonymous *Ordene de Chevalerie*.

CHAPTER 2

[1] 1884, republished by Chatto and Windus 1987, p. xv. For a detailed history of the earliest weapons up to the Roman period, look no further than Burton. Regrettably, the book-buying public in 1884 were not interested enough for the proposed second and third volumes of Burton's work ever to be published.

[2] See Malcom Vale, *War & Chivalry*, pp. 184-185 for a very interesting comparative table.

[3] These varieties of armour were probably differentiated in the 16th century. Most Lombard-manufactured Milanese armour of the 14th and 15th centuries had only a few plates that could be added for war; the wrapper for the armet, the pastron at the shoulder, and the grandguard over the couter. Combined, these pieces weigh perhaps 18 pounds. During the 14th century, we know of no interchangeable pieces, though specialised tournament armour is recorded. We do not, unfortunately, know precisely what it looked like or how it was made, though there is evidence of linen and canvas armour being employed in the medieval béhourd, where young bachelor knights competed against each other using batons of whalebone or ash. See Brian Price's forthcoming "*Pas d'Armes & Roundtables: Reenacting Medieval Feats of Arms.*"

[4] Literally the sword one was armed with, i.e. the sword you wore on your hip. This is the typical single handed sword of the medieval knight. These swords are commonly called broadswords today, despite the latter term not appearing in the language until the 17th century.

[5] As dated by Sydney Anglo in *The Martial Arts of Renaissance Europe* (2000), p. 326 (n).

[6] English funerary brasses and slabs show that English knights were usually equipped with longswords, from around 1325 to around 1460. This is made clear in *The Victoria and Albert Museum Catalogue of Rubbings of Brasses and Incised Slabs*, by Muriel Clayton (1968).

[7] The closest English treatise is probably the Harleian MS 3542, which is a short series of instructions regarding the "too honde swerde" (two-hand sword). George Silver also briefly covers the use of a longsword in his *Paradoxes of Defence*.

[8] in his definitive *Records of the Medieval Sword* (1991) Oakeshott identifies 22 medieval sword types, continuing Peterson's typology of Viking-era and earlier swords. Eight of these types classify what I would call longswords; types XIIa, XIII, XIIIa, XVa, XVIa, XVII, XXa and XX.

[9] These weights may seem surprisingly light to modern fencers used to blunt weapons. In my experience, a blunt longsword is about 3-400g (one lb = 454g) heavier than exactly the same sharp longsword, the difference being in the amount of metal removed from the blade in the sharpening process. Many of the cheaper modern weapons are absurdly heavy: I own one monster that is 2.7kg (nearly 6lb), and practically useless.

[10] The distinction between military and civilian is a modern one. In the fifteenth century, almost all classes of persons could be expected to go to war for their feudal overlord at some time. A more contemporary distinction is to refer to armoured/unarmoured fencing, or battlefield/street techniques. "Civilian" here refers to day-to-day, 'civil' conditions. Certainly anyone that could afford a sword and chose to wear one would be either a professional man-at-arms or of the knightly classes, and would therefore be schooled in what we would now call "military" arts.

[11] For evidence that the longsword was actually worn at the hip, refer to Clayton, and to the record of fifteenth century portraiture.

[12] Regarding cuts, the term used in the treatises is usually *colpi*, which is best translated as "blows". However, I prefer to refer to cuts, to emphasise the necessity of directing the edge properly, and making the "blow" actually "cut". See the relevant technical section for an expansion.

[13] The pros and cons of this will be addressed in the technical section.

[14] In England during the sixteenth century, the *spada da lato* was actually called a rapier by the men who carried them. However, the modern terminology by which historical weapons are classified, having the benefit of a historical overview, is in fact far more precise than the original.

[15] Evolution in non-scientific language implies improvement, so I do not mean to suggest that the 'advanced' smallsword "evolved" from the 'primitive' rapier. As circumstances (including taste and fashion) changed, so swords were adapted to them. I do not believe that the smallsword is the most refined, effective or sophisticated sword type. But it was the last civilian sword used in duels that was also carried for general defence and adornment. Remember that every major sword type is an excellent use of available technology to solve a particular problem. As the technology and the problems change, so does the sword type, and its method of use.

[16] There are exceptions to this. Fiore dei Liberi has a short section on the longsword used singlehandedly though it is too short to be considered as a complete method for that weapon. Some German manuscripts of the period also include the use of the *messer*, falchion or *düsack*, and it is implied that the same techniques would be used with a straight-bladed single-handed sword, but these texts were written *after* the appearance of the longsword, and the methods of using the *messer* appear to be based on its methods.

CHAPTER 3

[1] I am indebted to professor Ronnie Jack of Edinburgh University for checking a draft of this chapter, and making corrections, additions and suggestions for further research. Any errors and all opinions remain my own.

[2] The printing press was not invented until 1450, and its use took time to spread : the earliest known printed treatise on swordsmanship is Achille Marozzo's of 1536. All previous treatises were hand-written, and therefore produced in very small numbers at great cost.

[3] There are two full copies of essentially the same treatise; the one I use in this book, *Flos Duellatorum*, is known as the Pisani-Dossi manuscript, and was published by Francesco Novati in 1902. The other, called *Fior Battaglia*, and usually referred to as the Getty manuscript (because it is held in the Getty museum in Los Angeles, California) contains mostly the same illustrations, but the texts are quite different. Where the Pisani-dossi has short, cryptic verses, the Getty is far more comprehensively annotated with blank verse. For copyright reasons I will only be using illustrations from the Pisani-Dossi, but will compare the texts when necessary. There is a third, far less comprehensive copy in the Morgan museum in New York.

[4] There exists a centuries-old tradition of bestiaries, books that described the natural history of each animal as it was then understood, and included explanations of their Christian allegorical

meanings. They were very popular in their time, probably because they were used by clerics to explain Christian doctrine to the uneducated (remember that most books would have been written or copied by monks, who could exert whatever censorship they chose). No apparent distinction was made in the bestiaries between invented and existing creatures, and there was a remarkable continuity of interpretation for each symbol. There are at least 40 surviving examples dating from the twelfth to the fourteenth century (only the Bible and church service books survive in greater numbers, and we know of very few swordsmanship texts from before 1500). It is generally believed that all bestiaries derive from a common source, written in Greek in the second century AD, known as the *Physiologus*. The earliest extant example is from the eighth or early ninth century. My information on the bestiaries derives mainly from three works, which agree with each other very closely. T.H. White's *The Book of Beasts* (1954), accurately subtitled *a translation from a Latin bestiary of the twelfth century*, is a very accessible version of what appears to be a representative example of the genre. An excellent, conveniently alphabetised overview of each beast as they appear in the bestiaries is Florence McCulloch's *Medieval Latin and French Bestiaries* (1960). Wilma George and Brunsdon Yapp's *The Naming of the Beasts* (1991) goes into more detail regarding the history of the bestiaries, as well as providing interesting background and linguistic information, and excellent descriptions of the animals themselves. Further reading should include Beryl Rowland's *Blind Beasts: Chaucer's Animal World* (1971), and *On the Properties of Things: a Critical Text, John Trevisa's Translation of de Proprietatibus Rerum of Bartholomeus Anglicus* ed. M.C. Seymour (1975).

[5] There has been some disagreements in Western martial arts circles regarding this figure: is it a wolf (in modern Italian, *lupo*) or a lynx (in modern Italian, *lince*)? The original text is surprisingly clearly written: *louo cervino* (in the Pisani-Dossi), or *lovo cerviero* (in the Getty). In this period, u and v were used interchangeably: *lovo*, according to the *Grande Dizionario della Lingua Italiana* (1961) is an old Italian word for wolf. (It has survived in modern Spanish as *lobo* (v and b are practically interchangeable in Spanish), and shares its root with the French, *loup*, all derived from the Latin, *lupus*, meaning 'wolf'.) My research into the bestiaries indicates that in this period, a lynx was thought to be a type of wolf, though they had different characteristics. *Cervino* translates literally as 'deer-like', and means slender, lively or quick-witted. *Cerviero* is particularly associated with lynxes, and means having acute vision. A *lupo cerviero* is specifically a lynx. Lynxes in the bestiaries are usually spotted; so in the Pisani-Dossi, the text does not specifically imply a lynx, but the picture does, and in the Getty, vice-versa. It is reasonable to conclude, therefore, that the animal in question is a lynx, not a wolf. (I am indebted to Bob Charron and Rob Lovett for putting me on this track.)

[6] The equivalent page in the Getty manuscript has the same basic features, but the text is slightly different, and some features are missing, such as the naming of the guards in the lines that they cover. The animals are the same, and in fact drawn remarkably similarly, and carry the same symbols. The attribute of each is written differently, this time in Italian, not Latin, and in some cases translate differently. The tiger represents *presteza*, also swiftness, with the implication of readiness, or promptness. The lion represents *ardimento*, which comes from the same root as the English 'ardour', and means 'daring', or 'boldness'. The elephant, as before, represents *forteza*, strength. A detailed comparison of these two versions of the treatise would be a subject for a book in itself. For our purposes, an overview of the core meanings of the symbols and how they relate to actual fencing is all that is required.

[7] Professor Jack suggests that Prudence here derives from the second Homeric epic virtue "*sapientia*", which refers to practical wisdom in battle and was opposed to "rashness"; it would appear to be very close to military prudence.

[8] The translation of *Flos Duellatorum* I am working from is by Mr. Hermes Michelini of Calgary, Canada, under the auspices of the Knights of the Wild Rose, who have graciously given permission for its use in this book.

[9] Medieval Education, for those that could get it, was usually divided into seven subjects, in two groups. The TRIVIUM (the root of the modern English "trivial") was covered first and was comprised of the contingent/humane subjects: Grammar, Rhetoric, and Dialectic. Then

came the Sciences, the QUADRIVIUM, which consisted of Arithmetic, Geometry, Music, and Astronomy. See e.g. E. R. Curtius, European Literature and the Latin Middle Ages (1990).

[10] See for example Hale, J.R. (ed.) *A Concise Encyclopaedia of the Italian Renaissance* (Thames and Hudson, 1981)

[11] Mr. Michelini has "lightning" for *sagita;* I prefer "arrow", for four reasons: 1) the derivation of "tiger" from the ancient Persian for arrow; The river Tigris was named after the arrow because it was so fast-running. 2) The tiger is holding an arrow, as a symbol of speed. 3) The guard in the armoured combat section "sagitaria" is translated by Mr. Michelini as the guard of the arrow, and I have also seen it rendered as the guard of the archer; but never as the "lightning" guard. 4) The arrow was one of the more effective weapons of war at that time. More knights were killed by arrows than by lightning: so the tiger's message would include an encouraging suggestion that with Fiore's training, not even the arrow can overcome you.

[12] As in most treatises, Fiore is writing for right-handers; where necessary, the significance of the positioning must be interpreted with that in mind.

[13] It is interesting to note that Vadi previously refers to swordsmanship being like Music and Geometry, two of the Quadrivial subjects, subtly implying the necessity of swordsmanship as part of a gentleman's education.

[14] These translations from *De Arte Gladiatoria Dimicandi* are mine.

[15] As noted with Fiore, Vadi is writing for right-handers. The system should be reversed for left-handers: the bear is at the shoulder of the main sword-hand.

[16] From the bestiary tradition, the only relevant attribute is perhaps the way that bears fight bulls: they are supposed to grab their horns and bash their noses. This is an excellent parallel to good fencing (you must control your opponent's weapon, and destroy his weak spot) but probably coincidental.

[17] *Levoreto* is specifically a greyhound (there were several different breeds), which was used to hunt hares (a very popular Medieval and Renaissance sport), so the implications are that it is swift, deadly, trained, etc. They were particularly popular amongst the nobility, and very fashionable in the fifteenth century. Some breeds were fast enough to be used to catch birds.

[18] The original Italian is *ardito*, from the same root as *ardimento* as associated with the Lion in the Getty manuscript.

[19] This stanza is from Luca Porzio and GregoryMele's translation, *Arte Gladiatoria Dimicandi: 15th Century Swordsmanship of Filippo Vadi*, Chivalry Bookshelf (2003) page 88.

[20] These stanzas are also from Luca Porzio and GregoryMele's translation, *Arte Gladiatoria Dimicandi: 15th Century Swordsmanship of Filippo Vadi*, Chivalry Bookshelf (2003) page 88.

Chapter 4

[1] I am indebted to Maestro Jeanette Acosta-Martínez for her invaluable assistance in clarifying and correcting parts of this chapter. All errors and opinions remain my own.

[2] According to Stefan Dieke, in conversation, German longsword fencing is divided into *Zufechten* ("fighting towards"), *Handarbeiten* ("manual labour"), and *Ringen* ("wrestling"), which occur in the fencing distances as I have defined them.

[3] These ranges correspond with *misura larga* and *misura stretta* in rapier fencing theory (see Capo Ferro and countless other Italian rapier treatises for examples).

[4] These distinctions were first suggested to me by Maestro Andrea Lupo Sinclair; they are not specified in the treatises.

[5] This definition of *due tempi* is quite consistent throughout the history of Italian fencing.

[6] In the history of fencing *mezzo-tempo* has been variously used to mean many different things. The definition that I use comes from Vadi, Chapter 14, where his extensive description of it includes the following: "Of all the art this is the jewel,/ because at once it strikes and parries" (Porzio/Mele page 81). Vadi's suggestion that this is the "jewel" of the Art is one of the reasons that I emphasise counterattacks in my method.

[7] Porzio/Mele pages 77-78.

CHAPTER 5

[1] Or "rebated". This term refers to the point, and originally referred to the point being turned back on itself to be safe for thrusting. These days it refers to a pointed that has been made safe enough by rounding the end, or covering it with a leather or rubber blunt, or rebating.

[2] A "wall-hanger", as the name implies, is a decorative weapon intended only to hang on the wall. There are many companies making such pieces - much of it ghastly fantasy rubbish, and offensive to a trained swordsman. Good sword-makers of my acquaintance make even wall-hangers fit for combat: one also charges a "wall-hanging-tax", by asking a much higher price for the same sword if the buyer does not intend to use it!

[3] In the US and in some other countries, the legal climate discourages vendors from stating that a given piece of equipment is intended for any use other than display, so it might be difficult to coax a recommendation out of a vendor.

[4] In the US, tournament companies often address this problem the same way. They have one harness for practice, and one for use in tournaments. The idea is to have both function the same, but one is well-polished and much better crafted, while the other is rougher. The increasing use of tempered spring steels is in part reducing the need for multiple harnesses, but they are still expensive and relatively rare. See *Techniques of Medieval Armour Reproduction*, Brian R. Price (2000).

[5] At the time of writing, a Euro is worth almost exactly one US dollar, or about £0.65.

[6] See www.art-helsinki.com

[7] See www.swords.cz

[8] This is my private, independent opinion: I am not paid to advertise anyone's products.

[9] There is a move afoot, which I would like to encourage, to distinguish between in the terms "scabbard" and "sheath". A scabbard is rigid, usually made of wood covered with leather, while a sheath is a flexible, usually all-leather covering for the blade.

[10] This is a direct translation of the Finnish term for that plastic wire-wool that comes in sheets, often used for scouring pans. In the US, it is readily available under the trade-name "Scotch-Brite" by 3M.

[11] Sold under the trade name "Renaissance Wax", this formulation was created by the British Museum and is used in museums throughout the world on all kinds of metal, wood, leather, and even plastics.

[12] See Angelo Viggiani, *Lo schermo* (1575) for example.

[13] The Fédération Internationale d'Escrime, the international governing body of sport-fencing, which lays down very strict requirements for the equipment use in competitions. All fencing suppliers will know what you mean if you ask for an FIE approved mask.

[14] Proper medieval gauntlets are hard to obtain in the current marketplace. Generally, they come in two broad styles; "Finger" gauntlets, which have small plates defending each of the fingers, and "mitten" gauntlets, which use larger plates in bands to cover the finger area. Finger gauntlets themselves are broken down into two kinds; "scale" construction, and "gadling" construction, and they should have padding under the plates (such as leather or leather and felt) to further absorb impact. Mitten gauntlets, while more protective, are also more restrictive (though often significantly cheaper). As with most else, the skill of the armourer is of paramount importance when it comes to the overall function and protection that the gauntlets provide.

[15] "Mail" refers to armour made from wire rings linked together, often called "chainmail" by non-specialists.

[16] The earliest treatise on European swordsmanship, known as Royal Armouries Manuscript 1.33, dated about 1295, has the combatants wearing clerical robes, and gloves at all times. Gloves do not appear in Fiore's or Vadi's treatises outside the armoured combat sections.

[17] A gambeson is a padded jacket, often made from three to five layers of woollen cloth, covered in linen, or more accurately, quilted tubes, stuffed with padding (raw wool or cotton is perfect). There was no standard of terminology during the medieval period with respect to clothing or armour; this was referred to as a pourpoint, jack, gambeson, aketon and cote-armour, and

variances thereof. A plastron is a modern piece of equipment, and consists of a single piece of padding, protecting the chest, and slung on with straps (such as modern sport-fencing coaches use).

[18] See for example *The English Medieval Knight 1400-1500* by Christopher Gravett (2001): "shoes [were] designed to prevent skidding", (p. 9), which is supported by a lengthy quotation from the Hastings manuscript (from ca 1485).

[19] Amberger page 162.

[20] I have known some people attempt to cut down a tree with a sword. This is a stupid thing to do: the mechanics of a sword-cut are fundamentally different to those of an axe. Even a first-rate sword will break if you use it for inappropriate tasks.

CHAPTER 6

[1] It is important, particularly with single-handed weapons, to train on both sides, to balance the strain on the body and to acquire a deeper understanding of the techniques. This need not be done in the beginning, but consider it when you have mastered the basics.

[2] Much of my understanding of Fiore's footwork and bodymechanics was clarified by Bob Charron. I have worked primarily with the Pisani-Dossi; he with the (more textually useful) Getty. When we compared our interpretations, he was able to put the correct names to techniques I had inferred, and to add a great deal to my general understanding of Fiore's method. Interestingly, we had no major differences of opinion regarding interpretation, and we executed only a handful of techniques significantly differently.

[3] Precise instructions for footwork do not appear in the early swordsmanship manuals, though in the Getty manuscript, Fiore does distinguish between the advance, retreat, pass, half and full turn and diagonal step, and Vadi does hint at how to move correctly.

[4] Some other martial arts prefer to close the knee inwards, to protect the groin and femoral artery. This is perfectly valid, but is not a worthwhile compromise when longswords are involved, because it reduces your effective striking range without protecting a main target. Leg attacks are used, but are not emphasised in the way that, for example, the kick to the balls is in unarmed combat, and in any case, turning the leg in does not effectively protect against a sword-cut.

[5] This idea is not unique to European Martial Arts: there is an entire system of Chinese fighting techniques actually called *Pa Kua Chuan* ("Eight Directions Palm").

[6] This may surprise some martial artists: similar directional systems in other styles have the point of intersection in the centre of gravity of the swordsman.

[7] The lunge was not codified until the sixteenth century, so it does not appear as such in Vadi or Fiore's works, but many of the techniques appear to require attacks made with a step forwards of the front foot, with the blow landing at the same time as the foot: this is in effect the longsword lunge.

CHAPTER 7

[1] Various sword enthusiasts over the years have shown me many utterly ridiculous methods of holding a sword, including one hand on the pommel, the other on one tip of the crossguard; one hand on the pommel, the other gripping a side-ring: all of which make me despair of the intelligence, research, and practical experience of the fool suggesting it.

[2] I have known students who could execute excellent cuts after only a few repetitions, without really understanding what they were doing; and others that trained for months, well past 10,000 reps, without being able to reliably deliver a really good blow. However, those repetitions led to an understanding of the action that went far beyond just being able to do it.

[3] We recently had a guest in the salle from a British historical fencing group. He had never been taught to cut properly, and was having a great deal of trouble trying to cut in a relaxed manner. Somewhere inside himself he believed that power *must* be a product of effort. I was holding the tyre for him, and told him to hit it with his best shot. The result was a puny "thud". I then told him to forget about trying to actually hit it, and just do the technique the way I had told him, with no effort at all, just the lever action and the step powering the blow. He was shocked by the

"BOOM!!" that resulted. Without something to hit, he may never have been internally convinced that the correct technique was actually effective, and so might never have mastered it.

[4] I am indebted to Ville Virtanen for checking the physics in this section.

[5] I have not come across anything to suggest that this technique was or was not done in the longsword period. However, it is hard to believe that such a basic characteristic of sharp blades would be ignored.

[6] Vadi takes this idea to an extreme with his *spada in arme*, which has a leaf-shaped end sharpened over the last four inches, and a completely unsharpened blade from the hilt to the final four inches. This has led some people to suggest that normal longswords were only sharp near the tip: this is patently wrong, as the historical record shows. There was no standard degree of sharpness for a sword blade, and unfortunately many extant examples were re-sharpened by over-zealous curators in the nineteenth century. I think most longswords were reasonably sharp from cross to point, but few if any were razor-sharp at any point.

[7] In Italian, plural forms of nouns often end in i: so one *mandritto*, more than one *mandritti*, etc.

[8] It is commonly held that *mandritti* attacks are done with the true edge, and *roversi* with the false. That is generally true, and consistent with the treatises. However, I prefer to teach all cuts with the true edge to begin with because a) they work well that way; and b) they were done that way at least by Marozzo (*Opera Nova*, 1536) and Manciolino (*Opera Nova*, 1531), who state that all cuts are done with the true edge, and the rising cuts are also done with the false. When cutting with the true edge has been mastered, then it is useful to learn to cut in every line with the false edge. In free fencing, you will find that most *roversi* cuts are best done with the false edge, and most *mandritti* with the true, but you should not confine your training to only commonly useful techniques.

[9] "To properly understand and use [this Art], reason wants that I first reveal to you /the *rotare* (turning), principle of the sword./ Go with outstretched arms, bringing the edge in the middle of your partner/And if you want to appear great in the Art/ you then can go from guard to guard/ with serene and slow hand, / with steps neither long nor short." (Porzio/Mele page 70.).

[10]There is not space here to go into the controversy of cut over thrust; the argument is spurious. Swords are not, by and large, solely thrusting weapons (except the armour-piercing *estoc* or tuck, the smallsword, or the *epée de combat*), but very few extant swords are incapable of thrusting, the exceptions being usually executioner's swords or from the Viking or migration era. I agree with Vadi and Silver that the thrust is easily redirected (Vadi. "[a]nd when they [the thrusts] come at us/all blows make them lose the way"(Porzio/Mele page 66) Silver: "the force of a child may put it by" (*Paradoxes*, p. 21). Silver also states that "there is no fight perfect without both blow and thrust." (*Paradoxes*, p. 20). In any case, the thrust is a vital part of the swordsman's repertoire.

[11] As far as I am aware, the name for this thrust comes from the guard, *posta di dente cianghiale* (meaning boar's tooth guard, which looks like a contracted version of *porta di ferro mezana*). Boars were well known, and a favourite prey for hunters in medieval and renaissance Europe; their chief method of attack is a rising, ripping thrust with their tusks. The direct thrust from *posta di dente cinghiale*, which rises and rips like a boar's tusk (or "tooth"), is known as a boar's thrust. Incidentally, it remained sufficiently well known for Donald McBane to mention a version of it by the same name in his *Complete Sword-man's Companion* (1728).

[12] The word pommel derives from the same root as pummel. As the root is originally the Latin pômellum meaning "little apple," hence "knob", clearly the word pummelling meaning " hitting" derives from the practice of "pommelling": hitting with the pommel.

CHAPTER 8

[1] In my School we have quite a few left-handers. For their benefit, all the drills and forms we use have established variations for a cross-handed pair. These were originally called the "left-handed variations," until it was pointed out to me by a student that that was not accurate: a pair of left-handers do a mirror-image version of the drill, but when a right-hander and a left-hander

form a pair they sometimes have to do the techniques differently. These variations became known as the cross-handed variations.

[2] For an interesting overview of this see two articles in *SPADA* (Chivalry Bookshelf 2002), Gregory Mele's "Much Ado About Nothing" and Stephen Hand's "Counterattacks with Opposition."

[3] Most English dictionaries ascribe the earliest use in English to the seventeenth-century; and suggest the term to have come from a French or Latin root. However, they seem not to be aware that Italian fencing had a much greater influence in Britain at the time than the French. As Far as I am aware, the first use of the term in written English was in *Pallas Armata* (1639, by G. A.).

[4] Epigram from the beginning of Joe Simpson's *The Beckoning Silence* (2002).

[5] In the Getty manuscript, Fiore has this cut aimed from "jaw to knee." In Pisani-Dossi, it appears to be from the junction of neck and shoulder to the solar plexus. I prefer the latter, partly because it gives a greater safety margin in unprotected practice: the line to the junction of neck and shoulder is longer, and so overshooting your safety line slightly is less likely to result in a head contact. Head hits are far more dangerous than those to the shoulder.

[6] This drill originates with Brian Price, who developed it for his Schola Saint George *Introduction to the Medieval Longsword* course in California together with school Provost Robert Holland.

Chapter 9

[1] See, for example, the rules of the Salle as written by Sir William Hope in his *The Fencing-Master's Advice to his Scholar: or, a few Directions for the more Regular Assaulting in Schools (1692)*.

[2] From the Michelini translation.

[3] These two aspects of swordsmanship are interestingly paralleled in Eastern martial arts: in Japanese swordsmanship, for example, they are known as katsujin-ken ("life-giving sword") and setsunin-tō ("killing sword"). As Karl Friday points out in Legacies of the Sword (1997), "the "sword" in both cases refers not to the weapon itself but to its usage…When a combatant used force of will to overpower, immobilize, and strike down an opponent before he can react, this is called "setsunin- tō" … "Katsujin-ken" … involves drawing out the opponent, inducing him to strike, and then going inside his technique, countering it either at the moment of its origination [what we would call a mezzo tempo counterattack] or at the point of its most complete extension. [what we would call a stesso tempo counterattack]" (p. 31).

[4] See for example the tales surrounding Richard Marshal (son of the great Sir William the Marshal) in Michael Prestwich's, *Armies and Warfare in the Middle Ages: The English Experience* (1996) pp.1-2 (citing Roger Wendover's Chronicle). This can also be tested quite easily if you can afford to destroy good armour.

[5] That said, it was commonly done in medieval times, in tourneys and tournaments. However, the knights would been well aware of the realities of combat, so maintaining a proper martial attitude is unlikely to have been a problem.

[6] See Michael Prestwich, *Armies and Warfare in the Middle Ages: The English Experience* (1996) *pp.1-2*.

Bibliography

Main Treatises

Fiore de' Liberi da Premariacco, *Flos Duellatorum in armis, sine armis, equester, pedester* ed. (1409) ed. Francesco Novati (1902) (the Pisani-Dossi manuscript).

Michelini, Hermes, unpublished translation of *Flos duellatorum*.

Fiore dei Liberi da Premariacco, *Fior di Battaglia* (c.a.1410) (the Getty manuscript).

Filippo di Vadi, *De Arte Gladiatoria Dimicandi* (c. 1482-1487).

Porzio, Luca & Gregory Mele, *Arte Gladiatoria Dimicandi: 15th Century Swordsmanship of Filippo Vadi,* Chivalry Bookshelf (2003).

Supporting treatises and historical sources

Anonymous, *Ordene de Chevalerie.* (13th c.), published in *Ramon Lull's Book of Knighthood & Chivalry*, Trans. from the Middle English by Brian R. Price, Chivalry Bookshelf (2001).

Anonymous, Royal Armouries Manuscript I.33, (c. 1295), Trans. by Jeffrey L. Forgeng as *The Art of Medieval Swordsmanship: Royal Armouries MS I.33, A Facsimile & Translation of Europe's Oldest Personal Combat Treatise*, Chivalry Bookshelf, (2003).

G.A. (author's full name not known), *Pallas Armata* (1639).

dall'Agocchie, Giovanni, *Dell'arte di scrimia libri tre* (1572).

Alfieri, Francesco Ferdinando, *La Scherma* (1640).

King Rene d'Anjou, *Traictié de la forme et devis d'ung tournoy* (c.a.1470).

Capoferro, Ridolfo, *Gran simulacro dell'arte e dell'uso della scherma* (1610).

de Charny, Geoffrey, *Demands Pour la Joute, Le Tournois et La Guerre* (14th c.), translated by Steven Muhlberger in *Jousts & Tournaments: Charny and Chivalry Sport in 14th Century France*, Chivalry Bookshelf, (2003).

di Grassi, Giacomo, *Ragione di adoprar…*(1570). English translation Giacomo di Grassi, *true Arte of defence*, etc. (1594).

Hope, Sir William, *The Fencing-Master's Advice to his Scholar: or, a few Directions for the more Regular Assaulting in Schools* (1692).

Lull, Raymond, *Book of Knighthood and Chivalry*, (early 14th c.), published as above.

Manciolino, Antonio, *Se opera nova* … (1531)

Marozzo, Achille, *Opera Nova* … (1536).

McBane, Donald, *The Complete Sword-man's Companion* (1728).

Silver, George, *Paradoxes of Defence* (1599).

Silver, George, *Bref Instructions upon my paradoxes of defence*, in Matthey, Colonel Cyril, *The Works of George Silver* (1898).

Talhoffer, Hans, *Fechtbuch aus dem jahre 1467*, ed. G. Hergsell (1889).

Viggiani, Angelo, *Lo schermo* (1575).

Amberger, J. Christoph, *The Secret History of the Sword* (Multi-Media Books, 1999).

Anglo, Sydney, *The Martial Arts of Renaissance Europe* (Yale University Press, 2000)

de Bazancourt, Baron César, *Secrets of the Sword* (orig. 1862, trans. 1900, rep. Laureate Press 1998).

Burton, Sir Richard, *The Book of the Sword* (1884), (Chatto and Windus 1987).

Brown, Terry, *English Martial Arts* (Anglo Saxon Books, 1997).

Clayton, Muriel, *The Victoria and Albert Museum Catalogue of Rubbings of Brasses and Incised Slabs*, (HMSO 1968).

Curtius, E. R., *European Literature and the Latin Middle Ages* (Princeton University Press, 1990).

Friday, Karl, *Legacies of the Sword* (University of Hawai'i Press, 1997).

George, Wilma and Brunsdon Yapp, *The Naming of the Beasts* (Duckworth, 1991).

"Give a Dog a Bad Name" review of David Freeberg's <u>The Eye of the Lynx: Galileo, His Friends, and the Beginnings of Modern Natural History</u> in *The Economist*, February 22, 2003.

Gravett, Christopher, *The English Medieval Knight 1400-1500* (Osprey, 2001).

Oakeshott, Ewart, *Records of the Medieval Sword* (The Boydell Press, 1991).

McCulloch, Florence, *Medieval Latin and French Bestiaries* (1960).

Muhlberger, Steven, *Jousts & Tournaments: Charny and Chivalric Sport in 14th century France.* (Chivalry Bookshelf, Mar. 2003).

Prestwich, Michael, *Armies and Warfare in the Middle Ages; The English Experience* (Yale University Press, 1996).

Price, Brian R., *Techniques of Medieval Armour Reproduction* (Paladin Press, 2000).

Rowland, Beryl, *Blind Beasts: Chaucer's Animal World* (The Kent State University Press, 1971).

Seymour, M.C. (ed.) *On the Properties of Things: a Critical Text, John Trevisa's Translation of de Proprietatibus Rerum of Bartholomeus Anglicus* (Oxford Clarendon Press, 1975).

Simpson, Joe, *The Beckoning Silence* (Jonathan Cape, 2002).

"Two Bored Britons Battle in Armor", *Life* (International Edition) April 12, 1948.

Vale, M. G. A, *War and Chivalry: Warfare and Aristocratic Culture in England, France, and Burgundy at the End the Middle Ages* (University of Georgia Press, 1981).

White, T.H., *The Book of Beasts* (Jonathan Cape, 1954)

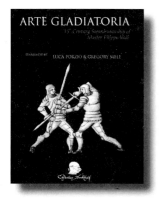

Chivalry Bookshelf

Publishers of New Works & Important Reprints

Western Martial Arts | Medieval History | Reenactment | Arms & Armour

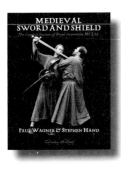
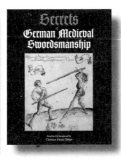

Write for your free catalog or find us online:

http://www.chivalrybookshelf.com

3305 Mayfair Lane | Highland Village, TX 75077
866.268.1495 toll free | 708.434.1251 worldwide | 978.418.4774 fax